UCHICAGO Consortium on School Research

RESEARCH REPORT MAY 2018

School Closings in Chicago

Staff and Student Experiences and Academic Outcomes

Molly F. Gordon, Marisa de la Torre, Jennifer R. Cowhy, Paul T. Moore, Lauren Sartain, and David Knight
with commentaries by Eve L. Ewing, University of Chicago and Douglas N. Harris, Tulane University

TABLE OF CONTENTS

1 Executive Summary

7 Introduction

Chapter 1
13 Overview of the School Closings Context and Process

Chapter 2
23 Planning and Transitioning into Designated Welcoming Schools

Chapter 3
33 Building Relationships and School Cultures in Welcoming Schools

Chapter 4
45 Impact on Student Outcomes

Chapter 5
57 Interpretive Summary

61 Commentaries

65 References

69 Appendices

ACKNOWLEDGEMENTS

The authors wish to acknowledge all of the educators and students who graciously let us into their schools, generously gave their time, and shared their experiences with us. The authors are indebted to each of the welcoming school leaders who agreed to participate in this study, and to the staff members who helped us schedule the site visit interviews, collect parent/guardian permission forms, and organize the student focus groups. We would also like to acknowledge the Chicago Public Schools for providing us with the administrative data that allowed us to do this work.

The authors also appreciate the many individuals who contributed to this report. We thank Maheema Haque for helping us code interviews, summarize qualitative data, and for contributions to the literature review. We were also fortunate to have the input of several people who provided constructive criticism along the way. We are grateful to our Consortium colleagues who read multiple drafts of the report and provided us with helpful suggestions for improvement, including Elaine Allensworth, Kylie Klein, Bronwyn McDaniel, Eliza Moeller, Jenny Nagaoka, Penny Sebring, and Jessica Tansey. Furthermore, prior to writing this report, we presented preliminary findings to several groups, including to members of our Steering Committee, the Consortium Investors Council, and program staff at the Spencer Foundation and the Chicago Community Trust. At each presentation, participants asked us thought-provoking questions and offered helpful suggestions for our analysis, interpretation, and subsequent writing. We also received vital feedback on the penultimate draft from two external reviewers, James Kemple and Mary Pattillo, who provided important points for us to consider as we finalized this report. In addition, we received extensive written feedback on the penultimate draft from several Steering Committee members, including Gina Caneva, Lynn Cherkasky-Davis, Lila Leff, Shazia Miller, and Beatriz Ponce de León. We thank them for their close read and thoughtful comments. We also thank our colleague Todd Rosenkranz, who conducted a thorough technical read of the report, and the UChicago Consortium's communications team, including Bronwyn McDaniel, Jessica Tansey, and Jessica Puller, who were instrumental in the production of this report.

We are grateful to the Spencer Foundation and the Chicago Community Trust for supporting this work and providing us with the necessary resources to conduct the analyses and write the report. We also gratefully acknowledge the Spencer Foundation and the Lewis-Sebring Family Foundation, whose operating grants support the work of the UChicago Consortium. Finally, we greatly appreciate the support from the Consortium Investor Council that funds critical work beyond the initial research: putting the research to work, refreshing the data archive, seeding new studies, and replicating previous studies. Members include: Brinson Foundation, Chicago Community Trust, CME Group Foundation, Crown Family Philanthropies, Lloyd A. Fry Foundation, Joyce Foundation, Lewis- Sebring Family Foundation, McDougal Family Foundation, Osa Foundation, Polk Bros. Foundation, Robert McCormick Foundation, Spencer Foundation, Steans Family Foundation, and The Chicago Public Education Fund.

Cite as: Gordon, M.F., de la Torre, M., Cowhy, J.R., Moore, P.T., Sartain, L.S., & Knight, D. (2018). *School closings in Chicago: Staff and student experiences and academic outcomes.* Chicago, IL: University of Chicago Consortium on School Research.

This report was produced by the UChicago Consortium's publications and communications staff: Bronwyn McDaniel, Director of Outreach and Communication; Jessica Tansey, Communications Manager; and Jessica Puller, Communications Specialist.

Graphic Design: Jeff Hall Design
Photography: Eileen Ryan
Editing: Katelyn Silva, Jessica Puller, Jessica Tansey, Andrew Zou, and Gina Kim

---

05.2018/PDF/jh.design@rcn.com

Executive Summary

Across the country, urban school districts are opting to close under-enrolled schools as a way to consolidate resources. Motivated by a reported $1 billion deficit and declining enrollments in depopulating neighborhoods, the Chicago Board of Education voted in May 2013 to close 49 elementary schools and one high school program located in an elementary school—the largest mass school closure to date. In order to accommodate the nearly 12,000 displaced students, Chicago Public Schools (CPS) designated specific "welcoming" schools for each of the closed schools.[1]

Although cost savings was the primary stated reason for closing schools, city and district officials saw this as an opportunity to move students into higher-rated schools and provide them with better academic opportunities. Underutilized schools, the district argued, were not serving students well. Supporters of the policy hoped that exposing students to better environments would generate academic gains and offset negative consequences.

There was strong, vocal opposition to the policy, including from the Chicago Teachers Union as well as from many families, students, and community groups. Most of the schools slated for closure were located in historically disinvested and primarily Black neighborhoods, with many of the schools serving areas of the city with high unemployment and crime rates. Critics feared that closing schools in these areas would destabilize communities and disrupt the lives of children and families, affecting their safety and security. Many also worried about students in welcoming schools and how they might be affected by large enrollment increases.

Prior studies on school closures have looked at the effects of closing schools on students' test scores, with a few studies looking at effects on student attendance and GPA. Evidence has shown that students experienced minimal or negative short-term effects beginning in the announcement year, with no long-term positive impacts.[2] Prior studies from the UChicago Consortium on School Research (UChicago Consortium) and others have shown that these effects were mitigated when students attended significantly higher-performing schools or had fewer disruptions.[3] A small number of qualitative studies have investigated how closing schools affects students, families, and staff. Findings reveal several potentially negative effects, including on student and teacher relationships.[4] Missing from prior studies is an in-depth understanding and comparison of the experiences of staff and students across multiple receiving schools. In addition, most studies have not looked beyond test scores to other kinds of relevant outcomes, such as mobility or suspension rates for displaced students or students in receiving schools. Policymakers need more information to understand the pros and cons, and implications, of closing schools.

---

1 Throughout the report we refer to district-designated welcoming schools as welcoming schools and other CPS schools where displaced students attended as receiving schools.
2 de la Torre & Gwynne (2009); Kirshner, Gaertner, & Pozzoboni (2010); Barrow, Park, & Schanzenbach (2011); Engberg, Gill, Zamarro, & Zimmer (2012); Brummet (2014); Bross, Harris, & Liu (2016); Larsen (2014); Steinberg, Scull, & MacDonald (2015).
3 de la Torre & Gwynne (2009); Barrow et al. (2011); Engberg et al. (2012); Kemple (2015); Bross et al. (2016).
4 South & Haynie (2004); Deeds & Pattillo (2014); Cole & Cole (1993); Seidman, Allen, Aber, Mitchell, & Feinman (1994).

In this report, we provide evidence of the short-term and multi-year impacts of the 2013 CPS school closures on students' academic, behavioral, and other relevant outcomes. We also illuminate the voices and experiences of the staff and students most directly affected by closures across six welcoming schools.

Our study addresses two primary research questions:

Research Question 1: How did staff and students affected by school closings experience the school closings process and subsequent transfer into designated welcoming schools?

Research Question 2: What effect did closing schools have on closed and welcoming schools students' mobility, attendance, suspensions, test scores, and core GPAs?[5]

To answer our research questions, we used a mixed methods design. This design allowed us to zoom in to illustrate what it was like for staff and students going through the school closings process in six welcoming schools, and zoom out to look at the impact of the policy on all affected students on a variety of outcomes.

Financial, utilization, and performance challenges faced by districts will likely result in more school closures in the future, in Chicago and elsewhere around the country. We hope findings from this report will provide helpful information for policymakers, educators, community members, families, and students to consider when closures are proposed.

CONTEXT
2013 School Closings in Chicago

In early December 2012, CPS identified a list of 330 underutilized elementary and high schools at risk for closures.[6] By February 2013, the district narrowed down the list to 129 elementary schools that were still under consideration. At the end of March 2013, CPS announced the final list of 53 schools and one program recommended for closure, and a final vote was set for the end of May 2013. Ultimately, 47 elementary schools and one high school program at an elementary school were closed at the end of the 2012–13 school year, primarily in the south and west sides of the city. Two other elementary schools were phased out the following year. Communities and schools had several occasions from December 2012 to May 2013 to attend meetings and hearings to advocate that their school be removed from the different recommended closure lists because of the staggered process for and the late announcement of the final list of school closures.

The district assigned students from closed schools to specific welcoming schools. These schools had to be within one mile of the closed school, higher-rated than the closed school (according to the district performance policy rating), and have enough available seats to accommodate students. The district invested resources in these welcoming schools, such as new or upgraded technology and extra discretionary funds for the first year, to enhance their learning environment and to prepare for the influx of students. In 14 cases, CPS determined that the closed school building should house the welcoming school, meaning that welcoming school staff and students had to relocate to the closed school buildings.

When the closures took place at the end of the 2012–13 school year, nearly 12,000 students were attending the 47 elementary schools that closed that year, close to 17,000 students were attending the 48 designated welcoming schools, and around 1,100 staff were employed in the closed schools. Thirty-six of the closed schools had a Level 3 rating ("on probation;" the lowest of three possible ratings), 11 had a Level 2 rating ("good standing;" the middle of three possible ratings), and none had a Level 1 rating ("excellent standing;" the highest of three possible ratings) in 2012–13. In contrast, 13 of the designated welcoming schools had an "on probation" rating, 23 had a "good standing" rating and 12 had an "excellent standing" rating that same year.

Sixty-six percent of students from closed schools attended the 48 designated welcoming schools. The rest enrolled in 311 other schools in the district.[7] On

---

5 Core GPA is the combination of grades in English, math, science and social studies classes.
6 CPS labeled a school as underutilized if the enrollment of the school was below 80 percent of its capacity, measured in fall 2012.
7 Six percent of students from closed schools transferred out of the district—a rate similar to prior years for the closed schools.

average, a designated welcoming school received 150 displaced students, accounting for 32 percent of their student population in fall 2013. However, some of the designated welcoming schools doubled in size, while others only received a small percentage of students from their corresponding closed school.

While the changes in the population of students and teachers suggest welcoming schools had to make major adjustments, to really understand what happened requires listening to student and staff experiences.

KEY FINDINGS
Student and Staff Experiences

To understand student and staff experiences, we identified six welcoming schools in which to conduct in-depth case studies, and interviewed educators and students in these schools.[8] The highlighted qualitative findings represent the key themes we found across the six case study schools and are based on the views, experiences, and perceptions of staff and students in these schools.[9]

- **School staff said that the planning process for merging closed schools into welcoming schools was not sufficient, resulting in staff feeling unprepared.** Once welcoming schools were identified, the district asked staff to produce written transition plans outlining how the schools would serve their new student populations. To help support principals in this process, the district provided them with principal transition coordinators. Planning for a merger of this magnitude was highly complex and involved a great deal of adaptation. School leaders said they did not know how to balance the need to plan with the recognition that the process, in reality, was unfolding with a high degree of uncertainty and ambiguity.

    Planning was also difficult because staff only had a few months and they did not always know how many of the closed school students would enroll in their schools, nor their final budgets. As the school year started, staff said they did not feel ready, and much of what had been written in the transition planning documents quickly became irrelevant as realities shifted.

- **Getting school buildings ready to receive students on time was challenging because the moving process was chaotic.** After the Chicago Board of Education voted to determine school closures at the end of May 2013, there was only one month left until the end of the school year. The new school year was scheduled to start on August 26, 2013, giving staff just two months to prepare the buildings, move supplies and furniture, and hire personnel for the 2013–14 school year. One of the largest impediments to getting ready for the school year was that the moving process was perceived as poorly managed. Roughly 95 school buildings needed to be packed up for the move. Staff said boxes were strewn throughout the school buildings and many staff reported that they lost valuable school supplies and materials during the move. As a result of the disorder and chaos, teachers said they did not have everything they needed for instruction or to support students at the beginning of the school year.

    In addition to having to deal with the clutter of moving boxes and the chaos of unpacking, staff also lamented that some of the welcoming school buildings were unclean, some needed serious repairs, and many upgrades fell short of what was promised or were delayed. Poor building conditions were seen as a barrier to preparedness, undermining community hopefulness about the transition. The inadequacy of the building space resulted in administrators and teachers spending a lot of time unpacking, cleaning, and preparing the physical space, rather than on instructional planning and relationship building.

- **Students and staff appreciated new investments in Safe Passage, technology, and resources.** To help support students in welcoming schools, the district provided extra funds and technology the first year of the merger. Some of the extra funds were used to

---

8 For more information about the qualitative methods, see Appendix A.

9 In addition to using interview and focus group data, we also analyzed survey data from the *My Voice, My School* surveys given to CPS students and staff yearly.

pay for welcoming events and activities, hire extra student support personnel, and/or add or boost academic supports for students. Many of these initial supports, however, were hard to sustain after the first year, according to school leaders, due to budget cuts in subsequent years and the end of the one-time influx of resources. However, some of the welcoming schools gained new STEM or IB programs, which the schools were able to maintain. One lasting support that interviewees appreciated was the expansion of the Safe Passage program, a program that hires Safe Passage workers to stand along designated walking routes during before- and after-school hours for added safety. Although school communities appreciated the expansion of Safe Passage, safety is still a major concern in many communities affected by school closures.

- **When schools closed, it severed the longstanding social connections that families and staff had with their schools and with one another, resulting in a period of mourning.** Those impacted by school closures expressed feelings of grief in multiple ways, often referring to their closed school peers and colleagues as *"like a family."* The intensity of the feelings of loss were amplified in cases where schools had been open for decades, with generations of families attending the same neighborhood school. Losing their closed schools was not easy and the majority of interviewees spoke about the difficulty they had integrating and socializing into the welcoming schools. Even though welcoming school staff and students did not lose their schools per se, many also expressed feelings of loss because incorporating a large number of new students required adjustments. Staff said they wished that they had more training and support on what it meant to welcome staff and students who just lost their schools. Interviewees wished that their grief and loss had been acknowledged and validated.

- **A lack of proactive efforts to support welcoming school communities in integrating the populations created challenging "us" vs. "them" dynamics.** Creating strong relationships and building trust in welcoming schools after schools closed was difficult. Prior to the actual merger, school communities said they felt as if they were competing with one another to stay open, which made accepting the loss that much more difficult. Displaced staff and students, who had just lost their schools, had to go into unfamiliar school environments and start anew. Welcoming school communities also did not want to lose or change the way their schools were previously.

To try to rebuild community within newly merged welcoming schools, staff held welcoming events, but these efforts often fell short. Tensions and conflicts arose, in part, because of differences in school cultures and expectations. Closed school staff and students, in each case, talked about feeling marginalized and not welcomed into the welcoming schools. Because of these feelings, staff and students said there was an increase in student fights and bullying, especially the first year of the transition. Over time, relationships began to improve. Staff expressed a need for more training and support in integrating school communities after school closures.

KEY FINDINGS
Student Outcomes

In order to determine the effects of school closures on student outcomes, we compared the outcomes trends of students affected by closures with students in similar schools that were not affected by any school actions.[10] These comparisons allowed us to estimate how the affected students would have performed had their schools not been affected. Using administrative data, we analyzed school transfer rates, number of days absent, suspension rates, reading and math test scores, and core GPA.[11]

Compared to students from similar schools, we found:

- **Students who were attending welcoming schools that relocated into the building of closed schools transferred out at higher rates just before the merger; mobility was not affected by school closures in subsequent years for either group of students.**

---

10 We focused on students who were in grades K-7 in spring 2013: 10,708 students from closed schools and 13,218 students from designated welcoming schools.

11 For more information about the quantitative methods, see Appendix B.

Students from closed schools transferred by necessity, while students in welcoming schools also left their schools for other district schools at higher rates in the summer prior to the merger. In fall 2013, 21 percent of the welcoming school students did not return to these schools. This number was almost 5 percentage points higher than expected given their prior school mobility and the mobility rates of other students in similar schools. The increase in the transfer rates was driven exclusively by students who were attending the 14 welcoming schools that had to relocate to the closed school buildings. In other words, when welcoming school communities were faced with having to move school buildings, families from the welcoming schools were more likely to look at other options.

- **All students affected by school closures had no changes in absences or suspension rates after the merger.** The number of school days missed by all students in our sample have been decreasing over time. Absences for students affected by school closures showed similar trends after the merger to the trends for students in comparison schools. Consequently, school closures did not affect the attendance rates of these students because absences changed at similar rates districtwide.

The percent of students suspended started to decrease in the 2013–14 school year, coinciding with the change in the CPS Suspensions and Expulsions Reduction Plan (SERP). These declines were evident for all students—those affected by closings and the comparison groups. The decline in suspension rates for students from closed schools was slightly more pronounced than the one for the comparison group, but differences were not significant.

- **Students affected by school closures did experience negative learning effects, especially students from closed schools.**
  • **The largest negative impact of school closures was on the test scores of students from closed schools; their scores were lower than expected the year of the announcement.** Similar to what other studies on school closures have found, student test scores in this case were lower than predicted given students' prior performance. Students' scores in the spring of the year of the announcement were roughly one and a half months behind in reading and two months behind in math. One reason for this might be that the announcement year was a disruptive year for many of these schools as they faced uncertainty about whether they would be closed. The district tried to avoid distractions in students' learning by waiting to announce the final list of school closures until after students took the state mandated tests (ISAT). However, students in closed schools still performed lower than the comparison group in the spring, even though their performance had been very similar in the fall and winter (measured by NWEA tests). Given the push to announce final closure decisions post-ISAT testing, it is not clear why there was a gap in ISAT test scores. The deviation in test scores in March between closed and comparison schools was somewhat unexpected as both were under the same threat of closing at the time the ISAT tests were given.[12]

  • **Students from closed schools experienced a long-term negative impact on their math test scores; slightly lower and short-term effects for reading test scores.** Reading test scores rose back to expected levels the second year post-closings for students from closed schools, but their test scores did not improve at a higher pace than students in similar schools. However, the gap in math test scores remained for four years post-closings, the last year in our analyses. The size of the effect was similar to the effect during the year of the announcement, which was approximately two months behind in math.

  • **Students from welcoming schools had lower than expected reading test scores the first year after the merger.** Reading test scores of students from welcoming schools were negatively affected the first year post-closing, scoring approximately one and a half months lower than expected given students'

---

[12] We ran some tests to try and understand whether there was any way to predict which schools would be on the final list of closures, but we found no distinctive data on these schools that would allow us or them to predict which ones were going to be on the final list.

prior performance. This was a short-term effect, as reading test scores rebounded the next year. Welcoming school students also had slightly lower than expected math scores, although this was not a significant difference.

• **Other learning measures, such as core GPA, were not affected immediately after closures, although we found some negative effects three and four years post-closures for students from closed schools.** Overall, core GPA improved slightly, especially the years after school closures for students. These increases initially occurred at the same rate for students affected by closures and their comparison group, but in years three and four post-closures (2015–16 and 2016–17), the core GPA for students from closed schools did not increase as much as the comparison group. The effects on core GPA were small, but negative, in years three and four post-closures. These negative effects were more pronounced for students who were in primary grades (3–5) in the announcement year (2012–13).

Conclusion

Our findings show that the reality of school closures was much more complex than policymakers anticipated; academic outcomes were neutral at best, and negative in some instances. Interviews with affected students and staff revealed major challenges with logistics, relationships, and school culture. A number of different factors played a role in why students did not benefit as much as hoped and why it was difficult for leaders and staff to create positive and welcoming learning environments, especially the first year of the merger. Closed school staff and students came into welcoming schools grieving and, in some cases, resentful that their schools closed while other schools stayed open. Welcoming school staff said they were not adequately supported to serve the new population and to address resulting divisions. Furthermore, leaders did not know what it took to be a successful welcoming school, suggesting a need for training that is more ongoing, along with time for reflections and targeted support. Students and staff appreciated the extra resources, technology, programs, and the expansion of Safe Passage, although they wished for longer-term investments because student needs did not end after one year. Staff and students said that it took a long period of time to build new school cultures and feel like a cohesive community. On the other hand, many of the negative concerns that critics raised did not materialize. Outcomes, such as absences and suspensions, were not affected by school closures. Our hope is that this report will add to our collective understanding of the effects of school closings.

Introduction

Districts across the United States, including Detroit, Philadelphia, New York, and Chicago, are closing schools, citing budget woes and population declines leading to a large number of under-enrolled schools. In May 2013, the Chicago Board of Education voted to close 49 elementary schools and one high school program located in an elementary school—the largest mass school closures to date.[13] In order to accommodate the nearly 12,000 displaced students, CPS designated specific "welcoming" schools for each of the closed schools.[14]

To identify which schools to close, the district focused on buildings with low enrollments. At the beginning of 2013, Chicago Public Schools (CPS) explained that the district had space for more than 500,000 students, but enrolled just over 400,000, calling it a "crisis of underutilization."[15] Because of this crisis, "resources across the district were spread too thinly and were not being used in the best interest of our students and school communities."[16] According to reports from the Commission on School Utilization, a group charged by then-CPS Chief Executive Officer (CEO) Barbara Byrd-Bennett to advise the district on school actions, severely underutilized schools carried "heavy academic, maintenance, and organizational costs which are borne by students, schools, and the district as a whole."[17] Academically, the commission argued, underutilized schools were more likely to have either extremely overcrowded classrooms or classes with multiple grade levels, and students in these schools were less likely to be exposed to art, music, or physical education classes.[18]

The city of Chicago has experienced periods of general population stagnation and declines since the 1990s due to changes in fertility/mortality rates, housing and labor market changes, and out-migration, including suburbanization and movement towards sun-belt regions of the country.[19] Recent losses are driven primarily by the out-migration of Chicago's Black population. From 2005–15, Chicago lost approximately 104,000 Black residents.[20] The current "crisis of underutilization" can be attributed to these population shifts as well as to various economic, housing, and education policy decisions made over the last couple of decades. Declines in school enrollment in areas impacted by closings have been attributed, in part, to a long history of economic and housing segregation, and racially biased urban planning decisions. Beginning in the late 1940s, the

---

13 Forty-seven elementary schools and one high school program closed at the end of the 2012–13 school year; the board voted to phase out two more elementary schools the following year.
14 Throughout the report we refer to district-designated welcoming schools as welcoming schools and other CPS schools where displaced students attended as receiving schools.
15 Chicago Public Schools (2013, January 10).
16 Chicago Public Schools (2013, February 13); Chicago Public Schools Facility Standards (n.d.).
17 CPS turned to an independent Commission on School Utilization to define and calculate building utilization rates. Commission on School Utilization Final Report (2013, March 6).
18 The Commission on School Utilization did not define what they meant by overcrowded classrooms or explain why underutilized schools may have had more overcrowded classrooms. Catalyst Chicago found that 12 percent of classrooms in underutilized schools and 4 percent of classrooms in schools that closed had above recommended class sizes (defined as more than 28 students). They also found that schools slated for closure did not have significantly more split-grade level classrooms than other schools across the district. About 14 percent of classrooms in closed schools were split-grade. Karp (2013, May 15).
19 Frey (2018, March 26); Anderson (2014); Goerge, Dilts, Yang, Wasserman, & Clary (2007).
20 Chicago Metropolitan Agency for Planning (2017a; 2017b).

city began erecting public housing units in primarily low-income Black communities leading to dramatic increases in the school-aged populations. The district, in turn, built more schools to accommodate the population growth in these concentrated areas.

By 1999, changes in the labor market, disinvestment in low-income neighborhoods, mismanaged and dilapidated buildings, and high crime rates led the Chicago Housing Authority to create the "Plan for Transformation." The Plan involved razing public housing units and relocating residents throughout the city, which contributed, along with other factors, to declines in the school-aged population in these areas.[21] While the city carried out the Plan for Transformation, there was also a big push to increase school choice. In summer 2004, Mayor Daley introduced Renaissance 2010, an effort to close low-performing schools and rebuild 100 new charter, performance, and contract schools by the year 2010. The stated purpose of the policy was to offer higher-quality school options for families.[22] However, out-migration and declining school-aged populations, paired with the effort to build new schools, helped give rise to decreased neighborhood school enrollments and underutilized schools, primarily on the south and west sides of the city.[23]

Policymakers projected that closing underutilized schools would save approximately $560 million in capital costs and another $43 million in operating costs over the span of 10 years.[24] Others expressed doubts in these savings; research on the sale of surplus buildings from 2005–12 in districts such as Philadelphia, Cincinnati, Detroit, and Washington, found that actual savings tended to fall well below projected valuations.[25] Of the schools closed in 2013, CPS had repurposed five of them, transferred three to the city for economic development, sold 26, and 10 buildings remained for sale as of April 2, 2018.[26] Information regarding the actual cost and savings from the 2013 round of school closures in Chicago has not yet been released or reported by the district.

Cost savings was the primary stated reason for closing schools, but the mayor's office and district officials saw this as an opportunity to move students from lower-resourced, lower-performing schools into higher-achieving schools. The prevailing assumption by policymakers was that under-enrolled schools were not serving students well. As Barbara Byrd-Bennett stated: "For too long, children in certain parts of Chicago have been cheated out of the resources they need to succeed because they are in underutilized, under-resourced schools ... By consolidating these schools, we can focus on safely getting every child into a better performing school close to their home."[27]

The district framed shuttering schools as an opportunity to provide students with better academic opportunities. As Mayor Rahm Emanuel stated, "I know this is incredibly difficult, but I firmly believe the most important thing we can do as a city is provide the next generation with a brighter future."[28] The nearly 12,000 displaced students would, in theory, experience a brighter future because they would be transferred to district-assigned, higher-rated welcoming schools with consolidated resources.[29] The district encouraged families to enroll their children into the designated welcoming schools, but families could opt to send their children to other schools with open seats. In fall 2013, 66 percent of the displaced students ended up enrolling into these designated welcoming schools. Approximately one-third of all displaced students enrolled in schools that had an "on probation" (Level 3) 2012–13 performance policy rating, with 21 percent enrolling in schools with "excellent standing" (Level 1) ratings. In contrast, 78 percent of the displaced students had attended closed schools that had an "on

---

21 For more information on Chicago's history of population increases and subsequent declines as well as the rise and fall of public housing units, see Hirsch (2009); Ewing (2016); Eads & Salinas (2014, December, 23); Dumke, Chase, Novak, & Fusco (2016, June 25); Chicago Housing Authority Plan for Transformation (n.d.).
22 Chicago Public Schools, Renaissance 2010 (n.d.). For more information on priority areas, see Catalyst Chicago (2007, December 1).
23 For more information on the effects of Rensaissance 2010, see Lipman & Haines (2007); Banchero (2010, January 17).
24 Chicago Public Schools (2013, March 21a).
25 Dowdall & Warner (2013, Feburary 11).
26 Belsha & Kiefer (2017, February, 12).
27 Chicago Public Schools (2013, March 20).
28 Emanuel (2013) as cited in Byrne & Ruthhart (2013, May 22).
29 Schools were rated on a scale of 1-3 based on the district's Performance, Remediation, and Probation Policy, the school accountability policy in place at the time of school closures. In the 2014-15 academic year, CPS introduced a new school accountability policy called School Quality Rating Policy (SQRP) for measuring annual school performance.

probation" (Level 3) rating, and the rest had attended a school with a "good standing" (Level 2) rating.[30]

The notion of closing down long-standing neighborhood schools is often met with fierce resistance. In a recent *Phi Delta Kappan* public opinion survey, 84 percent of Americans would rather opt to keep struggling schools open and provide support rather than close them down.[31] In Chicago, however, levels of support for school closures differed along racial lines; White residents reported higher levels of support, while Black residents reported lower levels of support. Differences were attributed to the disproportionate impact of closures on the Black community.[32] Although levels of support across the city varied, there was strong vocal opposition to the policy. Critics feared that closing schools would further threaten already economically fragile communities. As Karen Lewis, president of the Chicago Teachers Union, stated at the time, "We're going to have abandoned buildings. They destabilize the neighborhoods around them."[33] Most of the schools that were closed were located in historically disinvested and primarily Black neighborhoods. Many schools served areas of the city with high unemployment rates and high levels of crime. Opponents cautioned that closing schools would further disrupt the lives of children and families in affected communities. Compared to other students in the district, the students displaced by the 2013 round of closures were more likely to receive free or reduced-price lunch and special education services, and they were more likely to move residences and live in neighborhoods with high rates of crime and unemployment than students not affected by closures.[34]

Community members also warned district officials that sending displaced students to other schools in the neighborhood could be dangerous, as some students would have to cross gang lines in order to get to their new schools. To try to address these concerns, CPS expanded the Safe Passage program and hired Safe Passage workers to stand along designated walking routes during before- and after-school hours for added safety. Although more Safe Passage routes were added for students to get to and from the designated welcoming schools, opponents still worried about the possibility of increased fights and bullying inside and outside schools—especially between closed and welcoming student groups.

Furthermore, opponents of the 2013 round of school closings in Chicago worried about whether students going to the designated welcoming schools or other receiving schools throughout the district would actually fare better academically, socially, and emotionally once they were in their receiving schools. In addition, critics feared that the education of students already enrolled in receiving schools would be disrupted by the sudden inflow of large numbers of lower-performing displaced students, making receiving schools more vulnerable and a target for future rounds of school closures.

What Do We Know From Prior Research About the Effects of Closing Schools?

Research on the effects of closing schools, either elementary or high schools, is growing, but still sparse. Hence, the impact of such policies is not well understood. Most prior studies have shown that closing schools had minimal or negative short-term impacts on student test scores, with no long-term positive impacts.[35] The negative impacts on students' test scores often began the year of the announcement, at least in districts where the announcement took place before students took annual state tests.[36] The reasons behind the decline in students' academic performance during the announcement year are not well understood.

---

30 de la Torre, Gordon, Moore, Cowhy, Jagesic, & Nuynh (2015).
31 Starr (2016).
32 Nuamah (2017).
33 Yaccino & Rich (2013, March 21).
34 de la Torre et al. (2015).
35 de la Torre & Gwynne (2009); Kirshner et al. (2010); Barrow et al. (2011); Engberg et al. (2012); Brummet (2014); Bross et al. (2016).
36 de la Torre & Gwynne (2009); Barrow et al. (2011); Engberg et al. (2012).

In some instances, negative test score effects were mitigated in later years when students attended significantly higher-performing receiving schools.[37] A small number of studies have found positive effects involving closures where there is less disruption for students, such as phase-outs rather than immediate closures, particularly for high school phase-outs.[38]

In addition to studying the effects on test scores, a limited number of studies also looked at the impacts on other kinds of student outcomes. For example, a recent study of high school closures in Milwaukee found negative short-term effects on both GPA and attendance, but students bounced back over time.[39] Studies that looked into the effects of high school closures on high school graduation rates showed mixed results.[40] In addition, researchers also found short-term negative effects on attendance after elementary schools closed in Pittsburgh and Philadelphia.[41]

Policymakers rarely mention the effects of closing schools on the students in receiving schools, and prior evidence from a small number of studies is mixed. One study, for example, found no adverse effects on receiving school students' test scores,[42] while another found modest but significant negative effects on students' test scores in receiving schools.[43] In addition, a study of closed schools in Pittsburgh and Philadelphia showed that absenteeism increased for students in receiving schools as a result of closures.[44]

Very little research has been done on the experiences of families, students, teachers, and other school staff after transitioning to receiving schools. The few studies out there suggest that those impacted can experience a number of adverse academic, social, and psychological effects when schools close. For example, staff, students and their families going through a school closure process may experience uncertainty, apprehension, and resistance during this time period.[45] Student friendship networks can be lost when students switch to new schools.[46] Affected students may also experience significant shifts in peer relationships and relationships with teachers,[47] and feelings of safety and security.[48] When students transfer to new schools, their families can lose their social networks; parents may be less likely to talk to or connect with new parents, thus eroding social capital.[49] In addition, students who transfer to new schools because of mobility—forced mobility in the case of school closures, or during traditional transition periods (e.g. from middle school to high school)—can experience interruptions in their learning. This is due to changes in the kinds of curriculum, academic programs, or offerings that students are exposed to, as well as differences in instructional approaches and academic expectations.[50] These disruptions can sometimes result in academic,[51] behavioral,[52] and attendance issues.[53]

The Focus of This Report

Districts across the country are closing schools to save money, consolidate resources, and as a means to offer students better educational options. But to what extent does closing schools actually help students experience a "brighter future"? Critics warned of a number of possible adverse effects of closing schools—to what extent did students and staff in receiving schools experience any negative effects? Our convergent-parallel[54] mixed methods study helps answer these pressing questions by zooming in to illustrate what it was like for staff and students going through a school closings process, as well as zooming out to look at the impact of the policy on a variety of student outcomes.

In this study, we illuminate the voices of staff and students from six designated welcoming schools,

---

37 de la Torre & Gwynne (2009); Barrow et al. (2011); Engberg et al. (2012).
38 Kemple (2015); Bross et al. (2016).
39 Larsen (2014).
40 Larsen (2014); Kemple (2015); Bross et al. (2016).
41 Engberg et al. (2012); Steinberg et al. (2015).
42 Engberg et al. (2012).
43 Brummet (2014).
44 Engberg et al. (2012); Steinberg et al. (2015).
45 See: Witten, McCreanor, Kearns, & Ramasubramanian (2001); Ewing (2016).
46 South & Haynie (2004); Deeds & Pattillo (2014).
47 Cole & Cole (1993); Seidman et al. (1994); South & Haynie (2004); Kirshner et al. (2010); Deeds & Pattillo (2014).
48 Weiss & Kipnes (2006); Eccles, Lord, & Midgley (1991); Simmons & Blyth (1987).
49 Pettit (2004); Deeds & Pattillo (2014).
50 Gutman & Midgely (2000); Seidman et al. (1994).
51 Temple & Reynolds (1999).
52 Arcia (2007); Cook, MacCoun, Muschkin, & Vigdor (2008).
53 Eccles et al. (1991); Fink (2010).
54 Creswell & Clark (2011).

comparing experiences across these sites, and adding a nuanced perspective to the evidence base on school closures. Whereas most prior studies on school closures have focused narrowly on test scores or on attendance and GPA, in this report, we also provide evidence of the short-term and multi-year impacts of the 2013 round of school closures on students' academic, behavioral, and other relevant outcomes. Our study utilizes rich longitudinal datasets from CPS on individual students, teachers, and schools; annual survey data collected from students and teachers; and information from interviews with staff and focus groups with students.

Our study addresses the following primary research questions:

1. How did staff and students affected by school closings experience the school closings process and subsequent transfer into designated welcoming schools?

2. What effect did closing schools have on closed and welcoming school students' mobility, attendance, suspensions, test scores, and core GPA? [55]

Financial, utilization, and performance challenges faced by districts will likely result in more school closures in the future, not only in Chicago, but elsewhere around the country. As districts across the nation design closing policies, it is imperative to understand how these policies affect students, teachers, and administrators, including the potential benefits, challenges, and trade-offs. In this report:

- **Chapter 1** examines key elements of the school closings process and policy, including the timeline of events, as well as a description of how welcoming schools changed after the merger.

- **Chapters 2 and 3** zoom in on the lived experiences of students, teachers, and staff inside six designated welcoming schools to detail how the transition unfolded and what it was like to go through a school closings process.

- **Chapter 4** zooms out to look at the average impact of school closings on students coming from the closed schools and students who were already in receiving schools, including their test scores, GPA, suspensions, absences, and mobility.

- **Chapter 5** concludes with some implications of our findings.

---

[55] Core GPA is the combination of grades in English, math, science, and social studies classes.

CHAPTER 1

Overview of the School Closings Context and Process

At the end of the 2012–13 school year, the Chicago Board of Education voted to close 49 elementary schools and a high school program. This was not the first time that CPS had closed schools, but it was the first time that so many schools closed in one year. In 2002, three schools were closed for low performance. Since then, the district has continued to close schools almost every year, with up to a dozen closures happening at once in some years.[56] Low performance and low enrollment were the main reasons for these prior closures and, in fact, most schools shuttered in prior years could have been described as both.

Even though CPS has gone through the process of closing schools for many years, the 2013 school closures process was unique, not just in the unprecedented number of schools closed, but also in other important aspects. Even though some of those factors were not directly related to the school closures process, they indirectly affected the planning. For example, the academic year started on September 4, 2012 with a longer school year of 180 days. During the month of September, a 10-day teacher strike took place and consequently, the school year was extended until June 24, 2013. In addition, CPS named Barbara Byrd-Bennett its new CEO in October 2012. This chapter describes more in-depth the context and the steps during the 2012–13 school year leading up to the closure of schools and the transition of students into welcoming schools in fall 2013.

Leading Up to School Actions Announcement

By Illinois law, school districts planning any school actions, including closures and turnarounds, need to publish a draft of the guidelines that will be used in deciding those actions by October and announcements of any potential school actions need to be made by December 1 in the year before closures (**see Figure 1** for a timeline of key events during the 2012–13 school year). A few weeks after Byrd-Bennett was named CEO, CPS released a draft of the guidelines and created an independent Commission on School Utilization to gather community input and make recommendations on school actions guidelines. The Commission held a number of public meetings to gather input from the community and issued a report with its recommendations.

In November 2012, the district sought a one-time extension from the Illinois General Assembly to delay the announcement of possible school actions from December 2012 until spring 2013. The district released a statement saying that extending the deadline to March 31, "will give the commission the time it needs to rigorously engage communities and will provide schools with the time they need to focus on preparing their students for annual ISAT tests and avoid any distractions to student learning."[57] In exchange, the district agreed to a five-year moratorium on closings that ended in 2018. With the request granted, the school actions announcement was extended to the end of March 2013.

Selection and Announcement of Schools for Closure

Even though the final list of school actions did not have to be public until the end of March 2013, the district announced that 330 schools were underutilized in early December 2012, suggesting that schools on that list could be affected by school actions (a general term that can mean closure, consolidation, reassignment, boundary change, phase-out, or co-location).[58] This initial list included elementary schools, high schools, and charter schools, regardless of school performance. By

---

56 Vevea, Lutton, & Karp (2013).
57 Chicago Public Schools (2012, November 2).
58 CPS labeled a school as underutilized if the enrollment of the school was below 80 percent of its capacity, measured in fall 2012. Critics of the school closings policy questioned the formula the district used to calculate the utilization rates.

February, the district narrowed the list of 330 schools down to 129 elementary schools that were under consideration for closure. Using some of the recommendations from the report issued by the Commission on School Utilization, the district removed schools from the list if they were high schools or top-performing schools according to the district's accountability system.

At the end of March 2013, CPS announced a final list of 54 schools slated for closure. The district stated that community feedback and other recommendations from the Commission helped them to reduce the number of the schools on the list. In a CPS press release, they identified these criteria as "not closing schools that underwent a turnaround this year or are in buildings that were constructed or added additional permanent capacity in the last 10 years, and avoiding where possible sending students in a closed neighborhood school to a designated welcoming school more than a mile away." [59] The final vote took place at the end of May 2013 and the Chicago Board of Education voted to close 47 elementary schools, one high school program, and to phase out two more elementary programs within two years. Four elementary schools got a reprieve when the CEO withdrew her support for closing them and the Board of Education voted not to close them. [60]

Schools and communities had several occasions from December 2012 to May 2013 to advocate to be removed from the different lists, but the uncertainty created an unsettling environment. A first round of community engagement was hosted by the Commission on School Utilization in November and December 2012. [61] A second round was hosted by CPS from the end of January until the beginning of March with two community meetings per CPS network to gather information on individual schools that were on the February list. [62] In April 2013, a third round was again hosted by CPS and focused on the 54 schools on the final list. In addition, the district held state-mandated public hearings for each of the schools on the final list, presided over by independent hearing officers. All meetings were heated and contentious, with representatives from the schools and families presenting testimony to keep their schools open. [63]

After the Board of Education vote took place at the end of May 2013, there was barely one month until the end of the school year. The new school year was scheduled to start early on August 26, 2013, giving just two months to prepare the buildings, move supplies and furniture, and hire school staff to receive students for the 2013–14 academic year.

---

59 Chicago Public Schools (2013, March 21b). More schools were removed from the 129 list than those that fit these criteria. We found no additional information that would help us understand what other criteria the district may have used to determine the final list of 54 schools.
60 We could not find any official information about why these particular schools were removed from the list.
61 The Commission wrote a report with recommendations on school actions. Some of those recommendations were used as criteria to remove schools from the initial lists.
62 District-run schools in CPS are organized into geographic networks, which provide administrative support, strategic direction, and leadership development to the schools within each network. Community feedback from these meetings was used by the district to remove some schools from the 129 list.
63 Ahmed-Ullah (2013, April 25).

FIGURE 1
Timeline of Key Events of the 2012-13 Chicago School Closings Process

Pre-Announcement Phase

SEPT 2012
- **September 4:** Most schools started the academic year
- **September 10th:** 10-day teacher strike started

OCT 2012
- **October 12:** Barbara Byrd-Bennett was named CPS Chief Executive Officer
- **October 31:** CPS released draft school actions guidelines

NOV 2012
- A Commission on School Utilization was appointed by CPS CEO; it held six public hearings to gather input from community, the first round of community engagement

NOV 2012
- CPS announced the plan to seek an extention to the December 1 statutory deadline for school actions and a five-year moratorium on closures should the extention be granted

Decision-Making Phase

DEC 2012
- **December 5:** CPS announced that **330** schools were underutilized and at risk of closure

JAN 2013
- The second round of community engagement started; hosted by CPS to gather feedback on individual schools; 2 meetings hosted by networks from January 28 to March 4

FEB 2013
- **February 13th:** CPS announced a list of **129** elementary schools under consideration for closure, down from the initial 330

MAR 2013
- ISAT tests during this month
- **March 23:** The district recommended **53** elementary schools for closure and the closure of a high school program in an elementary school
- Letters were sent to parents with information on designated welcoming schools and the draft transition plans

APR 2013
- Third round of community meetings; 2 per school on the list
- State-mandated public hearings for each proposed school with CPS offering testimony followed by public comments

MAY 2013
- Updated transition plans for 9 of the schools after public hearings
- **May 22:** The Chicago Board of Education voted to close **47** elementary schools, **1** high school program, and to phase out **2** more elementary schools within two years. Four elementary schools did not close
- Enrollment fairs held in each closing school

Planning and Transition Phase

JUN 2013
- **June 24:** Last day of the academic year for students

JUL 2013
- Updated transtion plans were sent to families

AUG 2013
- **August 26:** First day of the 2013-14 academic year

Assigning and Preparing Designated Welcoming Schools

At the same time that district officials announced the closures list in March 2013, they also announced the list of designated welcoming schools, which would become the newly assigned schools for the students previously attending closed schools. These designated welcoming schools had to be:

- within one mile of the closed school,
- higher-rated than the closed school according to the district performance policy rating,
- and have enough available seats to accommodate the closed school's students.[64]

The second criterion was based on the 2012-13 performance policy rating that schools had and was available at the time the decisions were made. Three possible ratings were available under this policy—"excellent standing" or Level 1, "good standing" or Level 2, and "on probation" or Level 3—based on a number of different metrics that included test scores and attendance.[65] A school labeled as higher-rated by the district meant that either the rating was higher or, in cases when the ratings were the same, the welcoming school was higher-rated in most of the underlying metrics.[66] Thirty-six of the closed schools had an "on probation" and 11 had a "good standing" rating in 2012-13. In contrast, 13 of the welcoming schools had an "on probation" rating, 23 had a "good standing" rating, and 12 had an "excellent standing" rating that same year. Twenty-two of the closed schools were paired with a welcoming school that had the same rating.

The last criterion meant that the majority of the 48 designated welcoming schools (41 of the 48) were underutilized themselves and therefore included in the initial list of 330 potential schools to close; otherwise they would not be able to withstand a large influx of new students and staff.[67]

The district announced a series of investments and supports for these schools in order to help the transition of students and enhance their learning environments (**see Box entitled "Description of Stated Extra Supports and Resources for Designated Welcoming Schools"**). Some of those investments were directed to improve the facilities. In 14 cases, CPS determined, for different reasons, that the closed school building should house the designated welcoming school instead of investing in the welcoming school building. Therefore, the designated welcoming staff and students had to relocate to the closed school building.

Receiving an influx of students from closed schools meant that more teachers and staff would need to be hired at the welcoming schools. Around 1,100 staff were employed in the closed schools at the time of closures. Per the district's contract with the Chicago Teachers Union, to fill any open teacher positions at the designated welcoming schools, teachers from the closed schools who had tenure with "superior" or "excellent" ratings on the teacher evaluation system were eligible to follow their students if positions were open. Displaced teachers had to apply for these positions. If more than one high-rated tenured teacher from a closed school was eligible for a single position, seniority was one of the criteria considered during hiring.[68]

While the district encouraged families to enroll in schools before the school year was over, some displaced teachers and staff did not find out whether or not they could follow their students into the designated welcoming schools until late in the summer. In part, this was due to the use of student-based budgeting giving each school a fixed amount of money per pupil enrolled. Until there were enough students enrolled into the designated welcoming schools to fund a position, principals

---

[64] Busing was provided for students when the designated welcoming school was more than 0.8 miles from the closed school. Transportation assistance is offered to specific student populations (i.e., students with disabilities, students in temporary living situations, and NCLB-qualifying students) based on the CPS transportation policy.

[65] Schools earned points based on those metrics and an index was calculated based on the percentage of earned points. Level 1 schools received at least 71 percent of available points; Level 2 schools received between 50 and 70.9 percent of available points; and Level 3 schools received fewer than 50 percent of available points.

[66] See Chicago Public Schools (2012) for more details on how the district defined higher-rated schools.

[67] Eighteen of the 48 designated welcoming schools remained under the threat of closure when the district identified the list of 129 schools in Febraury 2013. These schools were eventually taken off the list at the end of March 2013.

[68] Agreement between the Board of Education of the City of Chicago and Chicago Teachers Union (2012, October 24).

Description of Stated Extra Supports and Resources for Designated Welcoming Schools

When district officials announced the list of the designated welcoming schools, they also described the investments they planned to make in these schools during the summer before and first year of the transition (2013–14).[A] This section describes the investments, extra resources, and supports CPS stated they were going to give to the designated welcoming schools.

Some investments were allocated to all designated welcoming schools and directed towards enhancing the learning environments:

- Air conditioning in every classroom and a library in every school
- iPads for students in grades 3–8 and new or upgraded technology
- Safe Passage routes with Safe Passage workers standing along designated paths to provide students travelling to and from designated welcoming schools with safer commutes
- Principal transition coordinators to help principals and school teams create detailed transition plans and support principals through the transition process. These principal transition coordinators were retired principals.

In order to support staff in helping students transition, the district planned professional development and other supports for all designated welcoming schools in spring and summer 2013, including: [B]

- Positive Behavior Interventions and Supports (PBIS) training to help schools set school-wide behavior expectations for students and staff
- Second Step curriculum training to implement in classrooms and help students build their social and emotional skills
- Restorative practices training to help prevent and respond to challenging behavior
- Social and emotional learning (SEL) and other trauma-informed supports for students through the Office of Social Emotional Learning and Lurie Children's Hospital

In addition, designated welcoming schools had access to new discretionary funds during the first year, part of the "Welcoming School Support Fund", to help with the transition. Some examples of how the district thought principals could use these funds included investing in programs to meet the unique needs of their students (e.g., tutoring, mentoring programs, counseling), hiring extra staff, and/or supporting welcoming events for families, students, and staff during the summer.

Depending on the specific needs of designated welcoming schools, CPS said certain schools could get additional investments and supports such as:

- Security and safety supports for inside the schools
- ADA accessibility
- Building upgrades such as painting
- Enhanced lunch rooms and food services to accommodate the larger student body

CPS also identified some areas of the city that were underserved in terms of access to high-quality programs. In order to address that, 17 of the designated welcoming schools in different neighborhoods got new programs in their schools. Ten schools got a Science, Technology, Engineering, and Math (STEM) program; six received an International Baccalaureate (IB) program; and one started a new Fine Arts program.

A Chicago Public Schools (2013, March 21b).

B Chicago Public Schools (2013, August 22).

could not hire staff.[69] Yet, there was uncertainty about how many students would enroll in the designated welcoming schools. The district allocated 89 percent of the student-based budget from closed schools to the designated welcoming schools before the beginning of the school year, and waited for final enrollment numbers to avoid taking some of the money away in September, in case the enrollment was lower than predicted.[70]

Merging Two Student and Teacher Populations

Previous research on school closings has focused on what happened to the students attending the closed schools after the closure, with a few other research studies unpacking the effects on students in the designated welcoming schools. In order to provide a fuller picture of the effects of the closings, we describe student and teacher populations in both closed and welcoming schools.

In a prior Consortium study, we showed that 94 percent of students from the closed schools reenrolled in CPS the following school year, which is comparable to district exit rates at those schools in earlier years.[71] Although the district designated a school for each closed school, it is an open enrollment system and families could choose to enroll their children into other schools with available seats. Among students who re-enrolled in CPS, 66 percent of displaced students enrolled into one of the 48 designated welcoming schools with the remaining 34 percent enrolling in 311 other schools across the district.[72] On average, the welcoming schools each received approximately 150 displaced students accounting for about 32 percent of their student population in fall 2013.[73] However, some of the welcoming schools almost doubled their size; in 12 of the 48 welcoming schools, 40 percent or more of their student population in fall 2013 came from closed schools. Meanwhile, other welcoming schools only got a small percentage of students from the closed school. For example, six welcoming schools had only about 10 percent or less of their student population in fall 2013 coming from closed schools. In contrast, the 311 receiving schools enrolled, on average, nine students from closed schools—accounting for only about 3 percent of their student population in fall 2013.[74]

Tables 1 and 2 show how the student and teacher populations in the welcoming schools changed after the merger by showing their characteristics in the year prior to the announcement (2011–2012 school year, column 2), and in the year after the closings (2013–14 school year, column 3). For comparison, the tables also provide information about the student and teacher populations in other elementary schools (columns 4 and 5). As reference, the tables provide student and teacher characteristics for the closed schools in the year prior to the announcement as well (2011–12 school year, column 1).

Prior to the announcement year, the closed (column 1) and welcoming (column 2) schools served students who were more likely to be Black and receive free or reduced-price lunch. These schools were also more likely to be lower performing than other schools in the district (column 4), and this is especially true for closed schools. The policy disproportionately affected Black students—88 percent of the students in closed schools were Black compared to 75 percent in welcoming schools and 36 percent in other schools. Students in closed schools at that time had average achievement levels that were 0.34 standard deviation units below the district average. They were also more likely to be old for their grade (23 percent of students from closed schools compared to 11 percent in other schools), and to qualify for free or reduced-price lunch (96 percent compared to 85 percent in other schools).[75]

Table 1 allows for a comparison of how the composition of welcoming schools changed after the closings (by comparing columns 2 and 3 from Table 1). Predictably, about half of the students in the welcoming schools had been in a different CPS school the year before 2013–14. While this is mostly mechanical because the students in closed schools had to switch schools, it makes

---

69 Karp (2013, October 7).
70 Chicago Public Schools Fiscal Year 2014 (n.d.).
71 de la Torre et al. (2015).
72 These schools did not receive extra supports and resources.
73 de la Torre et al. (2015).
74 One receiving school that was housed in a building with a closed school, but was not identified as designated welcoming school, received a large group of students from the closed school: 160 students. More than half of the other receiving schools served fewer than five displaced students.
75 A student who is old for their grade is a student whose age is over the traditional school age for their grade level. When students are old for their grade, it suggests that they have been retained in grade, either that year or in previous years.

TABLE 1

Student Characteristics by School Type

Student Characteristics	1. Closed Schools (Fall 2011)	2. Welcoming Schools (Fall 2011)	3. Welcoming Schools (Fall 2013)	4. Other Elementary Schools (Fall 2011)	5. Other Elementary Schools (Fall 2013)
Black	88%	75%	79%	36%	35%
Latino	10%	22%	18%	49%	49%
Free/Reduced-Price Lunch	96%	95%	94%	85%	83%
Students with Identified Disabilities	15%	13%	15%	11%	12%
Incoming Math Achievement (prior spring—standard deviation units)*	-0.34	-0.20	-0.29	0.04	0.04
Same School Prior Year	79%	79%	49%	80%	81%
Number of Students	13,048	15,486	23,297	239,290	243,884

Notes. Student characteristics were taken from fall enrollment at the beginning of each school year. Analysis was restricted to students in elementary school grades K-8.

* Test scores were standardized to have a mean of zero and standard deviation of one using the data from the 2012-13 year in order to be able to combine the scores of students in all grades. One standard deviation unit is roughly 30 ISAT points. On average, students have shown annual growth of 14 ISAT points in math. For example, students in closed schools were one-third of a standard deviation below the average student in the district. That translates to 10 ISAT points, close to a year of growth behind the average student.

explicit that there was a large disruption as the welcoming schools had to integrate two student populations and accommodate a much larger number of students. In contrast, in fall 2011, 80 percent of students in most elementary schools had been in those schools the year before.

Another large difference was in the average achievement levels of students since the welcoming schools took in students who were, on average, lower achieving than the students who were already in the welcoming schools. Prior to the merger, the welcoming population was scoring 0.20 standard deviations below the district average, compared to 0.29 below after the merger. These differences were not uniform across all the welcoming schools.

Figure 2 shows this visually. The blue dot represents the average ISAT scores for students from the welcoming schools in the announcement year, and the purple square represents the average ISAT scores for students in the closed schools that same year. In cases where the welcoming school students were higher scoring than the closed school students, the blue dot is higher than the purple square. The difference in the blue dot and purple square for each school is shown with the grey line. In 75 percent of the welcoming schools, the closing school students were, on average, lower performing than the welcoming students. It is worth noting that, in some instances, the average performance of students from closed schools was similar or even higher than the average performance of students from welcoming schools.[76]

Table 2 is similar to Table 1, but shows teacher characteristics. In the year prior to the closings announcements (2011–12), the teacher populations in the eventual closed and welcoming schools had a higher percentage of Black teachers than the other schools in the district, with fewer Latino and White teachers. About one-half of the teachers in closed and welcoming schools were Black compared to only about one-quarter of teachers in other district elementary schools. This disproportionality in the race/ethnicity of the teachers in closed schools was

---

[76] Note that where only one dot can be seen, the achievement levels were the same among students who came from the closed school and students already in the welcoming school.

FIGURE 2

Incoming Academic Achievement of Students from Closed Schools was Lower than Students at Many, but Not All, Welcoming Schools

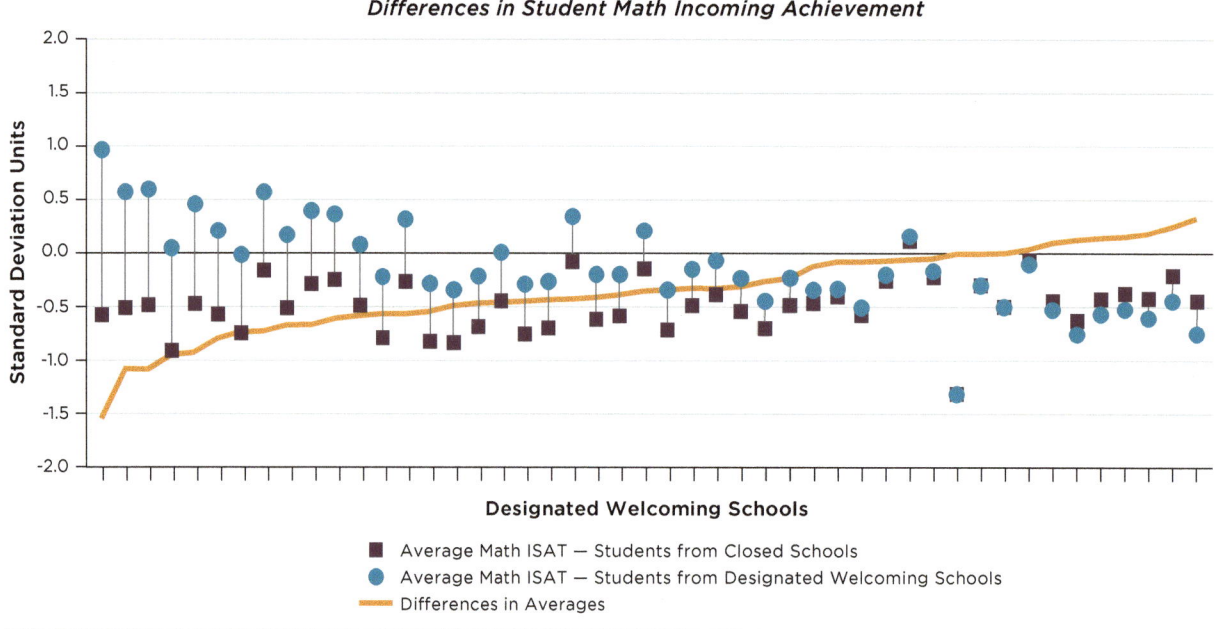

Differences in Student Math Incoming Achievement

Designated Welcoming Schools

- ■ Average Math ISAT — Students from Closed Schools
- ● Average Math ISAT — Students from Designated Welcoming Schools
- ─ Differences in Averages

Note: Based on spring 2013 ISAT data. Test scores were standardized to have a mean of zero and standard deviation of one using the data from the 2012-13 year in order to be able to combine the scores of students in all grades. One standard deviation unit is roughly 30 ISAT points. On average, students have shown annual growth of 14 ISAT points in math. To contextualize standard deviations, for example, a difference of one standard deviation means the lower scoring students were almost two years of growth behind the higher scoring students.

TABLE 2

Teacher Characteristics by School Type

Teacher Characteristics	1. Closed Schools (2011-12)	2. Welcoming Schools (2011-12)	3. Welcoming Schools (2013-14)	4. Other Elementary Schools (2011-12)	5. Other Elementary Schools (2013-14)
Black	54%	46%	50%	23%	22%
Latino	7%	9%	8%	21%	22%
White	31%	37%	36%	48%	51%
Female	84%	85%	85%	85%	83%
Graduate Degree	68%	68%	68%	67%	66%
National Board Certified	4%	4%	4%	7%	7%
Years Teaching in CPS	10.8	10.3	10.2	11.3	10.7
Teaching < 4 Years	21%	24%	24%	17%	21%
In Same School for 3 Years in a Row	72%	69%	40%	76%	69%
Number of Teachers	839	975	1,497	12,476	12,063

Notes. The data in this table is for all non-charter elementary school teachers, as charter schools do not provide personnel data to the district. Race data was not available for all teachers and that could affect the percentages reported here. Missing data: 5 percent of teachers in closed schools in 2011-12, 4 percent and 1 percent for welcoming schools in 2011-12 and 2013-14 respectively, and 3 percent and 1 percent for other schools in 2011-12 and 2013-14.

similar to the trend for students. In 2011–12, the teacher populations across closed and welcoming schools looked very similar to each other on many dimensions in addition to race/ethnicity, including the percent of teachers with a master's degree, as well as average years of experience in CPS. When it comes to teacher stability, around 70 percent of the teachers in the closed and welcoming schools in 2011–12 had been in the same school three years earlier (2008–09).

Table 2 also provides a sense of how much the teaching population changed after the closed and welcoming schools merged—that comparison is shown across columns 2 and 3. The demographics of the teaching staff across that time period were very similar in the welcoming schools, as were the qualifications. The major change was in the stability measures (whether teachers have stayed in the same school over a number of years), as well as the overall size of the teaching staff in welcoming schools. Only 40 percent of the teachers in the welcoming schools in 2013–14 were in the same school three years prior; this is to be expected given the influx of teachers from the closed schools. Even though it is to be expected, this still meant that the welcoming schools had a larger proportion of teaching staff that were new to the school than other schools in the district.

The next chapter describes the ways in which the closings affected the welcoming schools from the perspectives of the students and staff who lived through the merging of the schools. While the statistics on changes in the population of students and teachers suggest schools had to make adjustments, to really understand what happened requires listening to their experiences.

CHAPTER 2

Planning and Transitioning into Designated Welcoming Schools

Planning and preparing for merging two school populations was a complicated endeavor. Staff had to think about such things as reorganizing school space to accommodate large influxes of new students. Leaders had to plan for and anticipate changes in how students would move throughout the building, everything from scheduling of classes to lunch times. In addition, administrators had to consider staffing changes to utilize both existing and incoming staff from the closed schools. Furthermore, administrators had to think about the kinds of extra supports they needed to provide students and staff.

The timing for planning and preparing for this transition was tight. The earliest administrators and other staff could begin to plan for how to merge the old and new populations was once they found out they would be welcoming schools—around March 2013. However, final decisions on which schools would close were not made until the board voted at the end of May 2013. This left staff approximately three months to prepare for the merger. In this chapter, we used information obtained through interviews and focus groups to better understand what it was like for staff and students in welcoming schools during this planning and transition period. What kinds of initial transition efforts and supports were provided by district and school staff? How did this transition process and first year of the merger unfold in welcoming schools? Were there factors that helped or hindered the successful transition of students and staff into designated welcoming schools?

The aim of this chapter and the next is to illuminate the voices and experiences of those impacted directly by school closures and transitions into welcoming schools. Knowing more about the kinds of efforts made during this critical transition period, including what worked or did not work well, and the experiences of those going through a merging process after closures, is important for understanding the implications of school closings policies.

Staff perceptions of the support from district personnel for transition planning was mixed. By the time CPS formally announced the final list of closed and welcoming schools in May 2013, draft transition planning was underway.[77] In order to plan for a transition of this magnitude, the district mandated that all welcoming schools produce written transition plans and provided staff with planning templates to fill out. These templates included sections for staff to give information on how the welcoming schools would serve their new student populations, such as plans for students' social-emotional and academic learning needs, and more specific plans for students with diverse learning needs, English Learners, and students living in temporary situations. In addition, the templates included a section for staff to outline procedures and policies to ensure student safety and security. Lastly, welcoming school staff had to provide specific details in the appendices on professional development for teachers, structures, and resources that would be offered in the schools, and other information such as curriculum and cultural integration activities. A letter to parents and staff members in schools proposed for closure, along with draft transition plans, were sent in March 2013 and more detailed transition plans were made public on the CPS website in July 2013.[78]

Most of the welcoming school administrators in our sample assembled transition committees, teams, or task forces to help plan for the transition. To support administrators through this planning and transition process, the district assigned each welcoming school a principal transition coordinator.[79] Several of the principals in our six case schools valued the help they received from their principal transition coordinators. As one

---

77 Transition plans were drafted in March 2013 per the IL state law.
78 See: http://www.cps.edu/qualityschools/Pages/parents.aspx, a page for parents to search different closed school transition plans.
79 Principal transition coordinators were retired CPS principals.

Case Study Methodology

Case Study Sampling

We identified six welcoming schools in which to conduct in-depth case studies and make cross-case comparisons. These six welcoming schools had a range of school characteristics and outcomes so that we could capture a variety of transition experiences. Our sample included welcoming schools where at least 30 percent of the merged student populations came from the closed school, which was average. These schools had at least one administrator who was present the year of the merger. The final sample included schools on both the south and west sides of the city, with differing test score growth and performance levels (two schools were rated in "excellent standing," one in "good standing," and three "on probation" in the 2012–13 school year). Lastly, these six schools had a range of levels on school climate indicators such as teachers and students' feelings of safety in their schools. We also sampled a few welcoming schools that relocated into the closed school building. **Table A** summarizes the different characteristics of each of the case study schools (**see Appendix A** with more detailed information on the school sample and qualitative analysis).

Given schools' pre-closure trends (2009–10 to 2012–13) and controlling for the students being served in these schools, we predicted what the trends would be post-closure years in different outcomes using an HLM model. In the table, 'as expected' indicates that the actual school trends were similar to the predicted school trends. 'Lower than expected' indicates that the actual school trends were lower than the predicted trends. Lastly, 'higher than expected' indicates that the actual school trends were higher than the predicted ones. **See Appendix B** for a description of the data and the statistical models used to determine whether the outcomes were higher, lower, or as expected.

Starting in March 2016, we conducted 6–8 interviews at each school, including the principal,

TABLE A

The Sample of Welcoming School Case Study Sites had a Range of Outcomes on Test Scores and School Climate Indicators

	School 1	School 2	School 3	School 4	School 5	School 6
Welcoming School Relocated to Closed School Building	No	No	Yes	Yes	No	Yes
Percent of Closed School Students in Welcoming School*	40-50%	50-60%	40-50%	45-55%	30-40%	40-50%
Math ISAT Test Scores	Higher than Expected	As Expected	Slightly Lower than Expected	Higher than Expected	As Expected	As Expected
Attendance	As Expected	As Expected	As Expected	As Expected	As Expected	As Expected
Teacher Safety (Per Teacher Survey)	Lower than Expected	Lower than Expected	Higher than Expected	Higher than Expected	Lower than Expected	Higher than Expected
Safety Measure (Per Student Survey)	Lower than expected	As Expected	As Expected	Lower than expected	As Expected	As Expected
Classroom Behavior	Lower than Expected	As Expected	Higher than Expected	Lower than Expected	As Expected	Slightly Higher than Expected
Student-Teacher Trust	Lower than Expected	As Expected	As Expected	Slightly Lower than Expected	As Expected	As Expected

Note: *These ranges represent the percent of the student population in the welcoming schools coming from the closed school the fall of the merger, 2013. Ranges were used rather than actual percentages so as not to identify buildings. Given schools' pre-closure trends (2009-10 to 2012-13) and controlling for the students being served in these schools, we predicted what the trends would be post-closure years for different outcomes using an HLM model. In the table "as expected" indicates that the actual school trends were similar to the predicted school trends; "lower than expected" indicates that the actual school trends were lower than the predicted trends; and "higher than expected" indicates that the actual school trends were higher than the predicted ones. See Appendix B for a description of the data and the statistical models used to determine whether the outcomes were higher, lower, or as expected.

CASE STUDY METHODOLOGY.... Continued

assistant principal (if applicable), a student support staff member (e.g., counselor, social worker), and four teachers—two who transferred from closed schools into the welcoming schools and two who were teaching in the welcoming schools prior to the transition. In addition, we conducted two student focus groups in each school with seventh- and eighth-graders—one group with students who transferred from the closed school into the welcoming school and one group with students who had been at the welcoming school prior to it becoming a welcoming school. In total, we conducted 40 interviews and 12 student focus groups. In addition, we collected and analyzed school transition plans that were created by staff from each welcoming school in summer 2013.

We were unable to gather the views and perspectives of district personnel who played a role in the transition process. In 2013, we proposed to interview key district personnel involved in the school closings and transition processes. Our intended objective was to understand, from the district's perspective, how these individuals facilitated this process, including the supports, trainings, and information district personnel provided to schools and families. However, the Chicago Public Schools Research Review Board did not approve our request, raising concerns over confidentiality of interview participants due to the small number of central office leaders involved in the process. Subsequent district staff turnover also made seeking district perspectives not feasible for this study. Whenever possible, we used publicly available information and artifacts to understand how the district facilitated the process.

Analysis

The qualitative results in this report represent the themes we found across the six case study schools, highlighting the patterns that emerged in all sites. The experiences included in this chapter and the next represent the views of staff and students in these six schools only and therefore are not generalizable to the entire population of welcoming schools. Staff and students in welcoming schools not included in our analysis may have had very different experiences than the students and staff in our sample. At the same time, very clear and consistent patterns emerged across all six of our case study schools, despite being located in different parts of the city and having different outcomes, indicating that staff and students in other welcoming schools may have had similar experiences.

In addition to using interview and focus group data, we also analyzed survey data from the *My Voice, My School* surveys given to CPS students and staff yearly. We included these data to examine whether and in what ways the patterns found in the case study data existed more generally across other welcoming and receiving schools (**see Appendix B** with more information about survey data).

---

principal stated, *"[The principal transition coordinator] was extremely helpful because it was at least somebody on this level I could reach out and touch and so basically [the coordinator] became very familiar with this building"* (Principal, School 2). Similarly, another principal said that the principal transition coordinator served as their *"support system"* while they were writing the transition plans and accompanied staff to meetings at central office (Principal, School 6).

Not all principals in our sample said that their principal transition coordinators helped them during the planning and transition process. When asked to describe how the principal transition coordinators helped during the planning period, one principal stated, *"Not much.* *Very little. Very nice person but basically we did everything ourselves"* (Principal, School 4). Overall, the degree to which the principal transition coordinators helped during this transition period depended on the match between principal/school needs and the principal transition coordinator's skills and abilities. For example, one principal said that the principal transition coordinator provided a lot of encouragement but was *"not helpful in actually making it happen"* (Principal, School 5), something administrators in this school said they needed.

In addition to the principal transition coordinators, principals in the six schools talked about meeting regularly with network personnel during the transition planning time. During these meetings, principals and transition teams shared drafts of transition plans for feedback and received suggestions for improving their plans. One principal (School 1) referred to network personnel during this time as *"thought partners"* in the planning process. Another principal agreed that network personnel were helpful during the planning stages, saying, *"Whatever I needed, I called and I got it."* However, not all of the principals thought that central office or network personnel supported them adequately during this crucial period. For example, one principal (School 4) stated that central office staff asked their transition team to revise and reword their transition plan multiple times and that the process itself felt *"unorganized."* Overall, administrators and planning teams had varying experiences with the supports they received for planning purposes—from lots of helpful supports offered to some schools, to little help and support for other welcoming schools.

Staff said the transition planning process was insufficient to fully prepare for students in the fall. Planning is important for a complex process like merging a closed school into a welcoming school, but staff across the six schools reported that the process involved filling out a lot of paperwork—including the district transition plan template. However, staff recognized that the planning template they filled out represented what they thought they might be able to do, but did not often match what they could actually accomplish once the school year began. As one principal explained, the template was *"stationary"* and meant for a very specific situation, but the transition process itself was *"very organic"* and principals and staff had to be *"responsive"* to what was unfolding in real time. As they stated, *"So you can write all the plans you want, but when you get in there, you're not sure what's gonna happen, right?"* (Principal, School 1). Therefore, filling out the template ended up being more about compliance rather than a living document that was helpful or used once the school year began. As another principal stated, *"... people just sort of started filling in anything for compliance"* (Principal, School 5).

Part of the reason why the process was difficult to go through and plan for was because of the high degree of uncertainty involved in merging closed and receiving school populations. Planning for a transition like this, according to school leaders, was akin to planning for the unexpected. Leaders had to adapt in real time to the shifting and changing circumstances. Staff cited a number of reasons why the whole welcoming school planning process was flawed, including the truncated and rushed planning time, not knowing how many students or staff would be joining the welcoming school from closed schools, funding uncertainties associated with student-based budgeting, and uncertainties around planning for the physical accommodation of large influxes of new staff and students. Because of these challenges, many of the administrators said the planning directives and paperwork they had to fill out a few months prior to the merger were not helpful.

Furthermore, in two of the six schools, new administrators took the reins during the late summer of the transition year, but were not yet in buildings when transition plans were being developed by other staff members, including outgoing principals. These principals believed that not being a part of the planning process made it even more difficult for them to carry out the transition. As one new principal recalled about the transition plans they inherited, *"It wasn't a clear roadmap of what this welcoming school was supposed to look like"* (Principal, School 5). Overall, staff across each of the six schools said that once the school year started, much of what they planned for *"went out the window."*

Valuable supplies and materials were lost during the moving process, leading to significant challenges for staff. Staff across the six schools cited logistical issues that delayed their readiness to receive students in fall 2013. One of the largest impediments to getting ready for the school year was that staff lost valuable school supplies and materials during the move. At the end of the 2012–13 school year, all contents in the closed and welcoming school buildings had to be packed up, including all of the technology, books, furniture, etc. Some of the welcoming schools moved into closed school buildings, while others had to be packed up because administrators were moving classrooms around and rearranging space to accommodate staff and students coming in from the closed buildings. Roughly 95 school buildings needed to be packed up for the move at the end of the 2012–13 school year.

When staff arrived to the school buildings to get ready for the first day of school, administrators and teachers said that they could not find some of their school materials that they had packed up at the end of the last school year. Boxes were stacked in hallways and auditoriums and staff had to unpack and sort through what they described as a complete mess. In some buildings, administrators said that what they did get tended to be older supplies or equipment rather than what they had before the move. In addition, some staff lamented that valuable equipment was destroyed or lost during the transport. Teachers and staff in all six schools described that time period as *"chaotic."* As one teacher recollected while going through boxes:

"Nothing was left ... It was like they packed it up, they took it to a warehouse, and then they brought it all back and just put it anywhere. And so it was chaos ... So some of the things that I was used to finding, if I couldn't find it, I didn't have it anymore." (Welcoming school teacher, School 6)

In two instances, teachers from the closed schools believed that their old materials were offered to other schools within their network before they were offered to staff in the welcoming school. One teacher recalled after going to the closed school to try to collect supplies:

"Books were thrown all over the floors and everything was just in a terrible, terrible mess. It was a horrible mess. They [the closed school] used to have a really nice audiovisual system in their auditorium, so one of the teachers went to get it, and it had already been taken ... Everything was gone." (Welcoming school teacher, School 1)

District personnel, and in some cases students, were deployed to welcoming schools to help unpack. Staff also talked about family members and friends coming to help them unpack and set up to get the school ready for the start of the school year.

As a result of the disorder with the move and the loss of materials, teachers did not always have enough textbooks or supplies for students and in some instances did not have any books in particular subject areas at the start of the school year. Losing instructional materials and classroom supplies was disastrous for teachers, especially because many teachers use their own money to buy materials. Ultimately, teachers and staff in the six schools interpreted these losses as a sign that the district did not respect staff or care about the students in these schools. As one teacher explained, *"CPS doesn't care. They just don't care, and it shows"* (Welcoming school teacher, School 1).

Poor welcoming school building conditions hindered school staff from creating clean and inviting environments for their students and communities at the start of the year. In addition to having to deal with the clutter of moving boxes and unpacking, staff faced another logistical challenge during this transition time—some building upgrades were delayed and many staff perceived the welcoming school buildings as being unclean and/or needing serious repairs. For example, one school did not have doors on the bathrooms; in another, the bathroom stalls had no locks on them. One principal from a welcoming school that moved into the building of the closed school called the condition of the building *"filthy"* when they moved in.

Some buildings did get upgrades that first year, but most interviewees said they were disappointed in the district's building improvement efforts—either because they perceived them as poorly done and/or because the upgrades were not made in a timely fashion. For example, one principal stated, *"They half painted. They didn't really paint the corridors or anything. It was very tacky ... So we're still working on getting things in order as far as the building"* (Principal, School 4). Another principal shared similar sentiments, saying, *"All they [the district] did was put in air conditioners ... But they were dragging their feet, and the building wasn't clean. And I really think that was a systemic issue"* (Principal, School 6).

The inadequacy of the building space resulted in administrators and teachers spending a lot of time cleaning and preparing the physical space rather than focusing on instructional planning. For some staff, the fact that the buildings were not ready and the promised improvements were not made before the beginning of the school year felt like a big setback for them. As one principal from a school that moved into the closed school building explained:

"So I think that they could have had this building more prepared to receive us, to make it look like a new school for the current students that were at [the closed school]... and then the [welcoming school] students would feel like they were actually coming to some place that was nice and new and clean vs. coming into something that wasn't ready or prepared to receive us. I think that was the biggest downfall, the way we came into this building, which was a big setback for us." (Principal, School 4)

In addition to the challenge with accommodating a larger student population, in a few of the schools, students and staff were confused about why the district chose one of the buildings over the other. Some staff and students said that the other school buildings were preferable, meaning they were nicer, newer, or had coveted features such as gymnasiums or auditoriums. Because of this, several staff and students said they felt like they were sent to less desirable school locations, which made it even harder for them to accept the fact that their schools were shuttered.

Overall, poor building conditions were seen as a detriment to preparedness, undermining community hopefulness about the transition. These sentiments mirror research evidence, which suggests that it is difficult to create strong learning environments in facilities with poor structural quality.[80] Students and staff can feel discouraged and deflated when they have to teach and learn in run-down buildings. Several of the interviewees commented that because the buildings they ended up in were not well cared for, that it was another sign of the lack of respect on the part of the district and especially for families and children of color impacted by school closures.

Because of the large influx of students, scheduling and allocating the physical use of space was also a major challenge for administrators. In addition to the logistical issues outlined above, administrators also struggled with scheduling and planning for the use of physical space, given the large enrollment increases in these welcoming schools. In two of the schools, for example, there was not any room for libraries, despite the fact that all welcoming schools were promised a library. Students in these two schools confirmed this, saying things like, *"We don't have a library"* and *"We don't really have the library no more."* In two other schools, administrators had to repurpose gymnasiums for storage or other uses, prompting students to lament the loss of exercise space. As one closed school student explained, *"I felt very angry when I found out that we was coming over here … cause this [building] ain't got no gym room, ain't got no auditorium."* Administrators also talked about having to store supplies in classrooms and auditoriums. For those welcoming school administrators who moved into the building of the closed school, planning for the physical usage of space was even more daunting given that they moved into unfamiliar spaces.

Because all of the case study schools had large influxes of new students and staff, administrators and teachers talked about having to rework schedules, including everything from classes, to prep times, to lunch and testing schedules. For example, one assistant principal talked about the difficulty of scheduling students to take exams. They said, *"So instead of scheduling 200 students or 150 students to test, now I need to schedule for 500 and something students"* (Assistant principal, School 1).

Another teacher talked about all of the complexities that result from the merging of two populations. They explained:

"So I don't think any of us understood the impact of trying to learn 300 new students and dealing with so many [new] parents. And we had a hard time trying to figure out how could we get all of these kids fed in one day and everybody get recess and the bathroom situation, because there are like eight to ten classes per floor with only one girls and one boys bathroom. How are we gonna get all of these people in the bathroom throughout the day? So that was big. [Laughs] Scheduling was so much, and then providing preps for all of these teachers. So it was a big scheduling issue." (Welcoming school teacher, School 6)

There were additional district-level changes on top of school mergers, overwhelming staff in welcoming schools already experiencing tremendous changes.

---

80 Evans, Yoo, & Sipple (2010); Durán-Narucki (2008).

Planning for uncertainty and logistical challenges were not the only reasons why school staff said their schools experienced a rough transition year. Some welcoming schools switched networks and/or network chiefs and therefore, needed to adjust to new expectations. Some of these changes happened after the 2013–14 school year already began, so administrators had to further deviate from their original plans and adjust to the new mandates and expectations. In addition to network changes, some of the welcoming schools got new programs like IB or became STEM schools, which required further training and adjustments for staff. Furthermore, the district introduced a new discipline policy, encouraging schools to give out fewer out-of-school suspensions in favor of using more restorative justice approaches. In addition, this same year, the district began implementing Common Core State Standards and it was the first year of the full implementation of REACH teacher evaluations. Taken together, these were significant initiatives that schools had to undertake on top of becoming welcoming schools.

Staff and students appreciated the new resources and technology, although staff wished for more sustained resources and more training. Each welcoming school received extra funds to use the first year of the merger. Some of these funds were used to pay for welcoming events and activities. The remaining funds were used in various ways in each of the six welcoming schools. Two schools used the resources to hire extra student support personnel, including social workers and counselors to help with students' social-emotional needs. One school added security staff. For the schools that gained new STEM or IB programs, money was allocated to help build and support those new programs. Two schools added or boosted after-school academic support programs, and another bought supplies for students, including workbooks, pencils, etc.

Budget cuts in subsequent years and a lack of continuous funding meant that many of these initial supports were not sustained after that first year. Across the schools, interviewees said that budget cuts and the fact that the extra funds were only offered for one year meant that counselors and social workers that were hired had to be laid off.

In addition to the above, all welcoming schools received new iPads or other kinds of technology, such as laptops, smart boards or smart TVs. Staff across the schools agreed that the iPads, especially, were beneficial. As one administrator said, the iPads were *"definitely a huge lift for the school, definitely a good winning sell for the parents who were concerned about, 'What's different? What's gonna be new?'"* (Principal school 1). Students in the schools also appreciated the new technology. When asked about the differences between their closed school and the welcoming schools, one student said:

> *"So the difference is that the computers at the old [closed school], they were nice, but they were slow, and old, and rusty. We got iPads here, so that was much better. Then we got a whole computer lab where we have a lot of computers, just in case we don't have enough iPads."* (Closed school student, School 4)

While students and staff were happy to receive the technology investments, only staff from two of the schools said their school received support and training on how to use the iPads for instructional purposes. Staff wished for more technology support and training. For example, in one school, administrators had to upgrade and install software on all the new iPads, which took a great deal of time. One interviewee explained:

> *"We received a lot of iPads for any student third through eighth grade. Beautiful. Was something missing there? Yeah, of course, the training. You're going to give me a device where the students can use to connect to the internet, at least give us training to the teachers on how to utilize these beautiful devices to the benefit of the students."* (Assistant principal, School 1)

A lack of training and support meant that administrators and teachers did not always utilize the iPads and other technology to the fullest extent they believed possible.

Students and staff said they appreciated the expansion of the Safe Passage program. One lasting support that worked well, according to some interviewees, was the expansion of the Safe Passage program. One teacher said: *"Our Safe Passage people—power to Safe Passage—they were excellent as far as helping us out. We just wanted to make sure kids get home safe so they can come back the next day."* (Welcoming school teacher, School 4)

Another teacher in a different school echoed these sentiments, saying that the Safe Passage program was *"a good idea"* and that *"maybe it deters some kind of violence; you know if you see the yellow jackets [of Safe Passage staff] you might deter some kind of violence"* (Welcoming school teacher, School 3).

Students in focus groups also mentioned that they liked seeing Safe Passage workers along their routes to school. One student said:

> *"... cause like we know somebody's watching us, making sure we safe, but before, like before [the merger] we didn't have those people to like watch us."* (Closed school student, School 6)

Recent studies on the Safe Passage program indicated that the program is associated with reduced crime near schools that have routes and with improved student attendance in schools in these areas.[81]

Although students expressed that they felt safer walking to and from school because of the Safe Passage program, not all students reported feeling generally safer in their community. As several teachers and staff members across the schools said, gun violence and gangs are a danger and very present in the school community. One teacher talked about students now having to cross gang lines and travel further to get to school, which has led to some problems:

> *"There were also some issues where students had to cross certain boundary lines that normally they would not cross. I'm talking about gang boundary lines, neighborhood boundary lines, and there were some issues with that."* (Closed school teacher, School 5)

A teacher in a different school said something similar, commenting that when students are walking to and from school they *"have to be real careful because [they're] in two different gang territories ... So sometimes our kids get chased home because they stayed on one side vs. another around here."*

To see whether students' sense of safety walking to and from school was impacted more generally for students across other welcoming and receiving schools, we examined data from the *My Voice, My School* surveys both before and after the merger (**see Figure 3**). Overall, students in closed, welcoming, and other receiving schools felt less safe walking to and from school compared to students in other schools across the district, both before and after the school mergers. The year prior to the merger, about 63 percent of students in schools that became welcoming schools said they felt safe traveling between home and school, while a slightly higher percentage of closed school students (65 percent) and students in other schools that became receiving schools (66 percent) agreed or strongly agreed that they felt safe traveling to and from school. In general, the percentage of these students reporting feeling safe during their commutes increased slightly each of the four years after the merger.

In general, safety around the school was a much bigger concern for students at closed, welcoming, and other receiving schools both before and after the merger compared to students in other elementary schools across the district (**see Figure 4**). There was a very slight increase in the percent of students in affected buildings reporting feeling safe in the area around the welcoming schools the four years after the merger. The percentage of students in welcoming schools that agreed or strongly agreed that they felt safe around the school increased about three percentage points the year after the merger (from 51 percent to 54 percent), but dropped back to about 52 percent in 2014–15, and improved again to 54 percent the following year.

In trying to discern what school-level organizational processes helped or hindered the successful transition of students and staff into welcoming schools, we found many commonalities across the six schools. None of the schools felt prepared for the transition. Part of this had to do with the late date of the final decision, which left very little time to prepare. Another part had to do with the large degree of uncertainty around merging two school communities, combined with a rigid planning document and a largely unhelpful compliance-driven process facilitated by district personnel. In general,

---

[81] Gonzalez & Komisarow (2017); McMillen, Sarmiento-Barbieri, & Singh (2017).

FIGURE 3

There Were Similar Trends on How Safe Students Felt Travelling between Home and School After the Merger

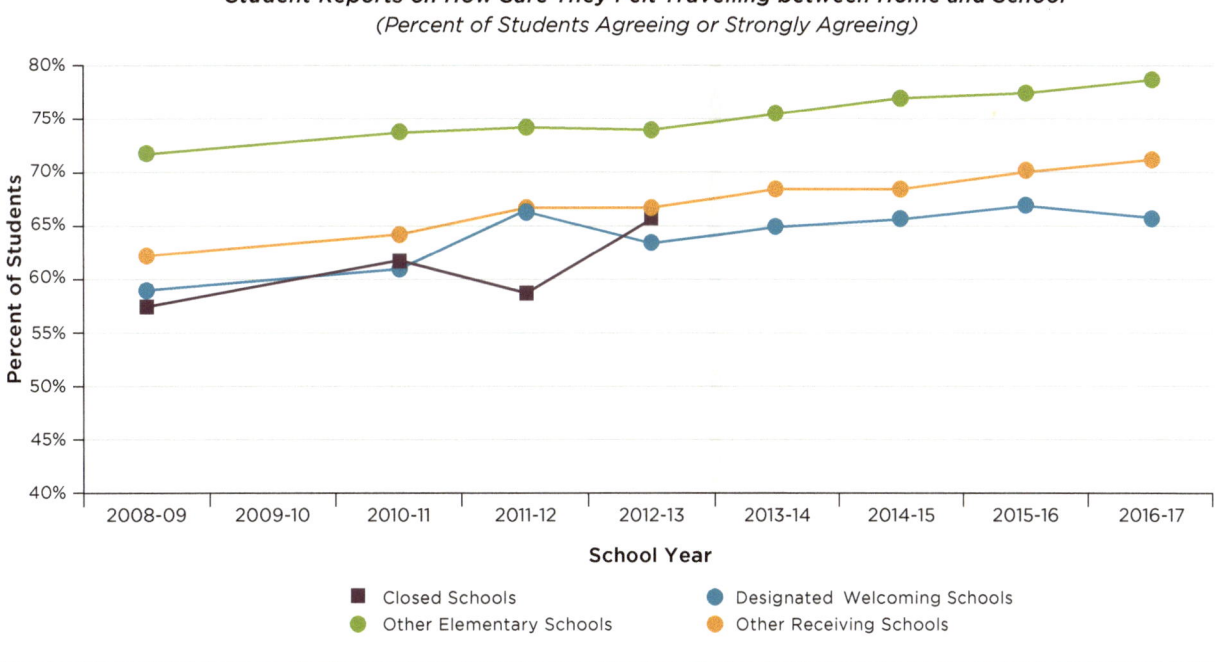

Note: This graph represents student responses on the *My Voice, My School* surveys. They reported on the school they attended in that particular year. See Appendix B for more details.

FIGURE 4

There Were No Major Changes in How Safe Students Felt Outside the Welcoming Schools after the Merger, but Safety is Still a Major Concern in Communities Affected by Closures

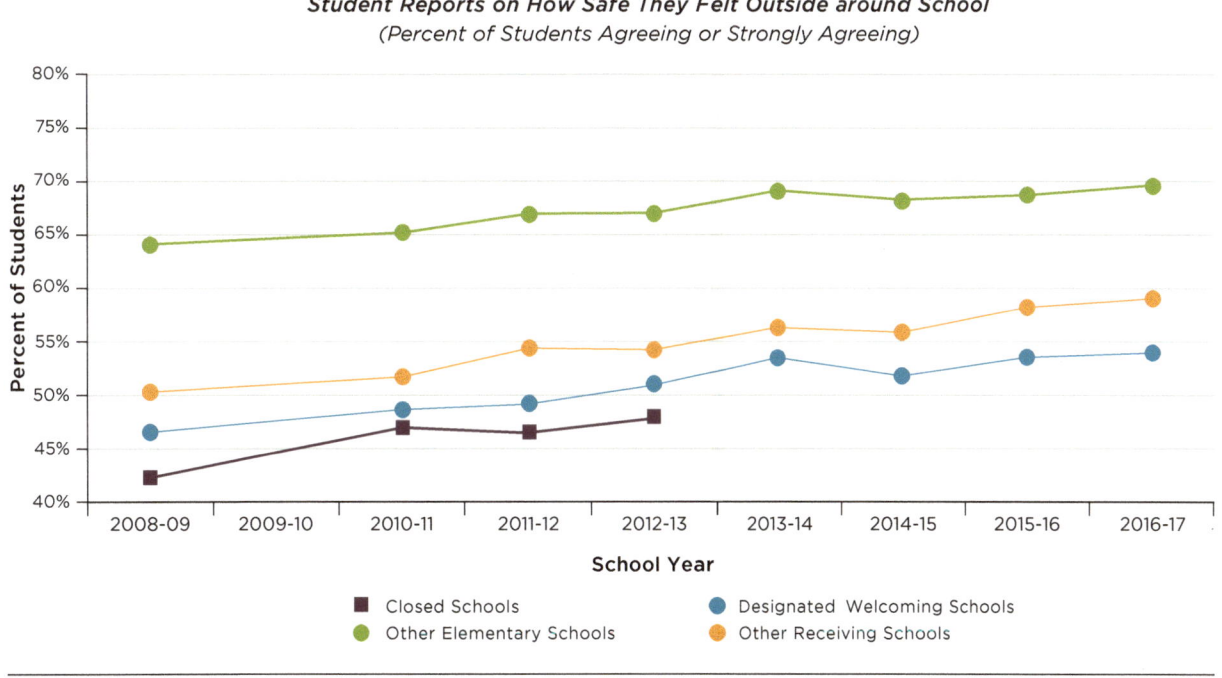

Note: This graph represents student responses on the *My Voice, My School* surveys. They reported on the school they attended in that particular year. See Appendix B for more details.

staff received very little guidance on how to prepare for large influxes of new staff and students. The things the district did provide, such as the principal transition coordinators and network personnel support, were not sufficient for schools to handle all of the organizational challenges. Delays in building preparation and the mismanagement of moving supplies and materials hindered schools from creating welcoming spaces for students and families. Administrators in these six sites said that they did not have a lot of power or control over processes that they normally have control over because of late district decisions, the lack of adequate building supplies and materials, as well as changes in networks and expectations. The majority of interviewees said they felt as though this transition process produced more losses for them, their schools, and their communities, than gains.

In the next chapter, we illustrate the ways in which staff and students in welcoming schools adjusted to the newly merged environments, focusing on their efforts to rebuild community.

Wished-for Supports: Planning and Logistics

When asked what planning and logistical supports staff and students wished they had during the transition year, they gave a variety of suggestions, including:

- More support and training on dealing with logistical changes associated with large increases in school size. Staff reported feeling overwhelmed by the large influx of students and struggled to adequately plan for the myriad of activities, from meals, to passing times, to scheduling, etc. Many of these logistical hurdles took much longer and required more time and thoughtful planning than anticipated.
- More care and effort in managing the move of supplies and equipment. Staff lost their schools', and in many instances their own, materials. Staff wished district personnel focused more attention on what teachers needed to teach effectively and showed more respect in teachers' ownership over their own materials.
- Greater attention and investments made to welcoming school facilities. Staff wished that buildings were ready and functional by the start of the school year. When students, families, and communities lost their schools, staff in welcoming schools wished they could have provided a more attractive, inviting, and welcoming space for their newly merged communities.
- More concerted, cohesive, and thoughtful effort by the district to bring principals going through this process together so that they could support one another in figuring out how to organize their schools and build a new school community.
- Longer term funding so that schools could continue paying for extra student support personnel and resources. Some staff said having to cut needed support staff and/or not upgrade technology after that first year was detrimental to their continued efforts to successfully merge communities.

CHAPTER 3

Building Relationships and School Cultures in Welcoming Schools

Merging closed schools into welcoming schools involved not only logistical and structural considerations as outlined in Chapter 2, but also the complex social and relational aspects of blending previously separate school communities. Schools are social organizations in which staff, students, and families interact with one another regularly, forming a network of relationships.[82] Strong relationships characterized by high levels of trust and collaboration are essential elements in well-functioning schools. Schools are much more likely to improve, for example, if they have strong professional community among teachers, trust, and parent and community engagement.[83] Teachers are more likely to stay in schools with trusting, supportive, and collaborative learning environments and students are more likely to learn and grow in these contexts.[84] When schools are closed and merged into another school, it can alter the delicate social dynamics and cultures of school communities. Different aspects of what makes a school a community can shift, including individuals' or groups' sense of membership or belonging, the degree of collaboration and communication, as well as the level of trust and influence individuals and groups have within the school.[85]

In addition to altering the social dynamics of schools, the merging process can also influence the culture of a receiving school. Schools have their own unique cultures and identities.[86] Every school, for instance, has its own norms, routines, goals, rules, and rituals. Some schools have assemblies to enhance school spirit, for example, while others have school creeds that students read together each morning. A school may have a mural representing the school's values or mascots that characterize the school's individuality. When schools close, those unique things are likely to be lost, and students and staff from closed schools mourn that loss. When they enter a receiving school, they may encounter a different school culture, resulting in tensions and conflicts in some cases.

Creating strong relationships and building trust in welcoming schools after schools closed was difficult. Displaced staff and students, fresh from losing their schools, had to go into unfamiliar school environments and start anew. Staff in receiving schools had to think about and plan for how to welcome newcomers from closed schools into their building. In this round of closures, enrollment in welcoming schools increased by approximately 150 students. They also had to figure out how to (re)build community and culture, while planning for and anticipating any potential issues that may arise from bringing together students from different neighborhoods. School leaders had to try to build trust with the community and help staff, students, and families build trust and relationships with one another.

In this chapter, we again use interviews with staff and focus groups with students from the six welcoming schools, as well as survey data to explore how staff and student relationships, trust, and school culture shifted as a result of merging closed schools into welcoming schools. The highlighted findings represent the key themes we found across the six case study schools, and are based on the views, experiences, and perceptions of staff and students in these schools. How did staff and students from closed schools adjust to merging into welcoming schools? What kinds of welcoming events and supports were offered and how did staff and students respond to them? What was the process like from the perspective of welcoming school staff and students? In addition, were there factors that helped or hindered the successful transition of students and staff into designated welcoming schools?

---

[82] Bryk, Sebring, Allensworth, Luppescu, & Easton (2010); Tarter & Hoy (2004); Goddard, Tschannen-Moran, & Hoy (2001).
[83] Bryk et al. (2010).
[84] Papay & Kraft (2017); Allensworth & Easton (2007).
[85] Osterman (2000); McMillan & Chavis (1986).
[86] See Schein (1996); Firestone & Louis (1999), for example.

The long school closing announcement process with schools fighting to stay open resulted in fractured communities. Interviewees said that the task of integrating closed and welcoming school communities was problematic from the start. During the year of the announcement, schools across the city were placed on the watch list in danger of being closed based on the district's underutilization formula. The long process of identifying schools in danger of closure, and hosting public hearings for schools to lobby to get off that list—intentionally or unintentionally—resulted in community divisions and rivalries. One principal explained what it was like during that time, saying, *"It was a year-long ordeal in uncertainty and fear for the communities, the teaching staff, the children. It was really a very, very impacted and traumatic situation to be in."*

The process was set up, according to interviewees, so that there were *"winners"* and *"losers"*. The *"winners"* in this case were schools that were taken off the closings list and the *"losers"* were schools that shuttered. Schools mobilized their staff, students, and families to attend the community hearings to fight to stay open. As the list was narrowed down over time, two or more schools within the same community remained on the list. Over time, it became clear to some schools that they may have to make the case that their school should stay open, while a different school in the community should close. As one interviewee put it, *"We knew that it was between the two schools,"* meaning that many staff knew towards the end that it would come down to either their school or another school near them. Several interviewees said that it felt like a competition between schools and that schools in the same neighborhoods were *"pitted against"* one another. As one principal put it, *"It remind[ed] me of The Hunger Games ... nobody wins in The Hunger Games."* As illustrated in the quote, nobody felt like they completely won in the 2013 school closures process.

According to interviewees, the whole closings process, including the long announcement period and the emotional toll of fighting to stay open, on top of the logistical issues during the transition planning, resulted in feelings of anger and resentment across communities. These feelings stemmed not just from having to go through a process of closure, but also because the communities affected most were already historically marginalized. As one principal put it:

"For me, it just shows systematically because this happened to children of color and I don't think people want to honor that and own it. But for me, it just showed me that canned systems just don't show that they care for our children of color ... I think parents realized that they weren't respected. They went out and they protested and prayed and begged to keep their schools open to deaf ears ... I think everyone has a welcoming school war battle."

Rebuilding school communities, trust, and relationships in newly merged welcoming schools after what many characterized as a *"battle,"* was daunting for all involved.

To try to integrate the two populations, welcoming schools hosted welcoming events, but these events often fell short of building community. Staff across all six schools hosted welcoming events such as picnics, bowling parties, carnivals, meet and greets, and festivals intended for the closed and welcoming school communities to get to know one another. However, staff said that many of these efforts did not result in meaningful community integration. For instance, one school hosted a meal for staff to get to know one another at the beginning of the school year, but staff who came from the closed school said that they sat separate from the welcoming school staff and did not mingle. One of the teachers described what it was like at the gathering, saying:

"It was an effort. But, to me, it was just a meal because basically I had so many other things going on in my mind. They [welcoming school staff] weren't really, at that time, trying to interact with us—the staff over there, even to the point that in a room all of us sat on one side and all of them sat on the other side." (Closed school teacher, School 6)

Both welcoming and closed school students also said that they did not really talk with the other group of students at these events and many wished that staff had been more hands-on in helping the two student groups get to know each other better prior to the merger. For instance, one student said that staff, *"could have had us like work more like with different people that we normally don't talk to just to get the experience of how it be when we go to [welcoming school]"* (Closed school student, School 4).

A student from a different school had a similar suggestion, saying, *"I wish they like had something like a open house so we can get to know everybody before we came so we'd feel less isolated on our first day"* (Closed school student, School 5).

To many of the interviewees in our sample, welcoming events solidified the divisions between these closed and welcoming school communities rather than the commonalities. For example, a student in one focus group said, *"They [school staff] threw us a [party], so like so we could connect [with the closed school students]... I didn't really like it too much"* (Welcoming school student, School 5).

However, when school leaders had strategies for building common culture, staff and student relationships appeared to develop faster. One of the six schools was more successful in terms of trying to integrate the two communities than the others. In School 3, welcoming school staff hosted a number of *"get to know you"* events at a local community center and facilitated team-building activities for staff and students. Teachers said that their administrators were very intentional about building relationships during these events by making sure that welcoming school and closed school staff, students, and families sat together and actually talked with one another. As one teacher from the closed school recalled:

"We had a lot of team building things at [community center], actually ... That was nice because it was a nice meet and greet and was kind of fun. You'd walk in and there would be like a [closed school] table of people, then there would be the [welcoming school] people. [The principal] was like, 'This isn't going to work. We need to split you up.' [The principal's] like, 'Let's put you by grade level.' I thought it was a really good, smart mix." (Closed school teacher, School 3)

Students from School 3 also said that the events and integration efforts helped them to get to know the other students. One student explained:

"For me, it was pretty cool because like the last couple of days we had left in the school, some of our [welcoming school] students were like coming to visit [us]. So we actually got the time to start getting to meet them. It was pretty good ..." (Closed school student, School 3)

In this case, teachers mentioned the strong role that administrators played in making sure their welcoming school co-created a new community together. One teacher from the closed school said that administrators were *"very supportive"* and created *"common ground for both schools."* Another teacher in the school explained the importance of strong leadership during this transition time:

"When we first transitioned, they [administrators] were everywhere. It was like you turned around and there was someone from the administration team, whether it be the principal, the vice principal, and counselors, whatever. Their presence was known. They were making sure to not only be seen for the teachers, but also for the students, and then for the parents." (Closed school teacher, School 3)

In addition to welcoming events, school leaders tried other ways of integrating the staff. For example, some of the leaders intentionally paired teachers from both schools into grade-level teams to facilitate cross collaboration. Others tried reassigning teachers to teach different grade levels so that they would be part of newly blended teacher teams. In some cases, intentional pairing helped bring teachers together to form connections. In other instances, however, these kinds of changes exacerbated some of the existing conflicts and tensions in the buildings.

Although in most instances welcoming events were not very successful at building community, some teachers and staff members thought that welcoming events may have helped students recognize familiar faces during the first few days of the school year, even if they did not interact at these gatherings. They said:

"With the children, I believe it just gave them a sense of they knew faces when they came in. They didn't know the name; they knew the face. 'But, weren't you the one when we came? When we came to your school didn't I see you playing?'" (Welcoming school teacher, School 3)

It was difficult for closed school staff and students to want to build new relationships because they were still mourning the loss of their former school communities. For displaced staff and students, losing their schools felt in many ways like a death. Participants in the study expressed their grief in multiple ways, but most used familial metaphors, often referring to their closed school peers and colleagues as *"like a family."* In this way, the loss of their schools had an emotional and destabilizing effect. For instance, one displaced student explained their grief this way: *"I feel like I lost a family member"* (Closed school student, School 6). They used the terms *"brothers and sisters"* to describe closed school friends and *"stepmother and stepfather"* to describe closed school teachers saying that these relationships subsequently *"disappeared."* The frequency with which interviewees used familial metaphors to explain their loss suggests that the strong connections and attachments to schools remained long after they closed.

The intensity of the feelings of loss were amplified in cases where schools had been open for decades, with generations of families attending the same neighborhood school. In many of these buildings, a high percentage of teachers had been teaching in these schools for years (**see Table 2 in Chapter 1 on p.20**). When these institutions closed, it severed the long-standing social connections families and staff had with the school and with one another. Interviewees expressed this disconnection again using familial metaphors. For example, a teacher from the same school as the student above described what it felt like to be in the closed school building right after the announcement was made that it would close, saying:

> *"I looked at it like a divorce, like I was the child and my parents were breaking apart, they were leaving ... you just felt that feeling like something was going to happen; things were not going to be the same."* (Closed school teacher, School 6)

These sentiments of loss are consistent with place attachment theory—the idea that people become attached to specific places, much like they become attached to friends and loved ones.[87] People become attached to places, in part, because they evoke personal memories, especially in places where meaningful events occur. The physical structure of a school, for example, can evoke strong memories, as many milestones take place in schools. Perhaps more importantly, families, teachers, students, and staff in schools form strong bonds and networks with one another. Because of these connections, schools foster social cohesion and serve as stabilizing forces in a community. When schools shut down, it can have a destabilizing effect because connections can be severed leaving those affected experiencing grief and loss. Ewing (2016) called this phenomenon institutional mourning, defining it as "the social and emotional processes undergone by individuals and communities facing the loss of a shared institution." She argues that institutional mourning has a greater impact on socially marginalized groups because the loss "amplifies their reliance on the institution or its relative significance in their lives" (p. 151).[88]

In the cases where welcoming schools moved into the building of the closed schools, mourning came not from losing a physical building, but instead from feelings of being taken over by another school community. Closed school teachers talked about feeling *"invaded"* when the welcoming school moved into their building. As one closed school teacher explained:

> *"... imagine you coming into your home, you're sitting in the bathroom, all of a sudden somebody comes into your house, a stranger you don't know. How do you feel? You feel invaded, you feel your space [has been] taken away."* (Closed school teacher, School 3)

Welcoming school administrators and staff confirmed these sentiments, saying that when they moved in it felt like they were *"invading someone else's home"* or that it felt like *"moving into another person's home."* These quotes illustrate that welcoming school staff understood that these buildings used to *"belong"* to a different school community.

Leaving their closed schools behind—either physically or metaphorically—for a new school environment was not easy for the closed school community. The majority spoke about the difficulty they had integrating and socializing into the welcoming schools. As one teacher who came from a closed school said of the merger, *"... it was very difficult. And a lot of us don't accept change well. When you get out of your comfort zone, you don't like it"* (Closed school teacher, School 2).

---

[87] Scannell & Gifford (2010); Manzo (2003).

[88] Ewing (2016).

Welcoming schools staff and students also mourned the loss of what their schools were like before the merger. Many welcoming school participants were reluctant to embrace becoming a welcoming school. Although they did not lose their schools per se, interviewees spoke about not wanting to lose or change the way their schools were previously. For instance, prior to becoming a welcoming school, one administrator said that their school *"was more close, meaning it was more like family"* (Administrator, School 1). In another case, a welcoming school student said that it was hard to accept the fact that new students and staff were joining the school because they, *"liked how the school was already"* (Welcoming school student, School 4). Staff and students often cited larger class sizes, increased enrollment generally, changing buildings in some cases, and incorporating students and staff from unfamiliar neighborhoods with greater social-emotional demands, as reasons why the welcoming school did not feel as close-knit as it was before the merger. As one welcoming school teacher stated, *"It's just we lost something big. [Welcoming school] was always, to me, a pillar in this community. We had a really good reputation."* However, that changed after the merger, according to this teacher.

These sentiments are consistent with prior research on what happens relationally when organizations or companies go through a transition or merger process. Dominant group members' social identities can shift because a new social group is formed by merging the "old" group with a "new" incoming group.[89] When applied to school settings, these findings suggest that welcoming staff and students who had strong ties and group identities associated with their school prior to the merger no longer felt like they identified with the school in the same way post-merger. The shift in group identity associated with a merger can affect the stability of organizations. Students from welcoming schools were more likely to leave these schools and change to a different school just before the merger (**see Figure B.1 in Appendix B**). The increased turnover at welcoming schools further exacerbated feelings of loss.

At the same time, not all interviewees were upset about the idea of becoming welcoming schools. Some students, for instance, said they were ready and excited for the change. For example, after finding out the school was becoming a welcoming school, one student said, *"It was rejuvenating, basically refreshing. It's a new start from all the drama and stuff"* (Welcoming school student, School 3). Another student expressed a level of excitement about the change, saying,

> *"When I heard that our school was becoming a welcoming school, I didn't mind that they [closed school students] were gonna come here because I thought that I was gonna make new friends …"* (Welcoming school student, School 1)

Some staff embraced becoming a welcoming school as well, but wished that they had more training and support on what it meant to welcome staff and students who just lost their schools. As one staff member said, *"Being a welcoming school could be a positive thing, but we didn't really know how to be a welcoming school"* (Welcoming school teacher, School 2).

Closed school staff did not always feel welcomed into their new school environments, exacerbating divisions. Fragile relationship dynamics were aggravated further by feelings of not being welcomed into welcoming schools. Closed school staff mentioned multiple reasons why they felt they were not welcomed into the new schools. Some, for instance, said that they were actively labeled as *"closed school"* teachers that first year—solidifying their identity as separate from the rest of the staff. This labeling exacerbated existing "us" against "them" dynamics. Some closed school teachers referred to themselves as *"transplants"* or *"outsiders"* because that was how they said they were treated. As one teacher who came from a closed school explained, only a small handful of the welcoming school staff really welcomed closed school staff into the building: *"We did not fit in here, we were not really welcomed in this school, the way that we should've been. It was not our fault that we were sent here; it was not by choice"* (Closed school teacher, School 1).

Others talked about being physically segregated within school buildings. For example, teachers in one case said that they did not meet very many welcoming

---

[89] Van Leeuwen, Van Knippenberg, & Ellemers (2003).

school teachers during the first year, and that it was on them as individuals to meet their colleagues. As one teacher reported, *"To be quite honest with you, if you did not go out of yourself to meet somebody, you would have no idea who they are"* (Closed school teacher, School 6).

In a couple of instances, closed school staff said that they felt like the welcoming school staff looked down upon them because their school closed. This was because the district said that when schools closed, students would be assigned to "higher-performing" welcoming schools. Therefore, some staff in welcoming schools treated closed school teachers as inferior. As one of the closed school teachers recalled:

> *"'Your school closed, so you were a failure. You guys didn't make the cut and we did.' Even with the lead teacher it was that attitude … I had to inform her that I was a tenured teacher. I probably had more years than she had, or just about the same. It was that thing that they were talking down to us like, 'You don't know what you are talking about. This is how we do it.' That's how it was directed."*
> (Closed school teacher, School 6)

In some cases, closed school teachers felt like the parents also questioned the closed school teachers' abilities because there was a belief that teachers who came from the closed schools weren't good teachers. As one teacher explained, *"We were here because we were no good, you know—I guess they had to give us a job, and so that's why we were here"* (Closed school teacher, School 1). In another case, welcoming school staff said disparaging things about the closed school. For example, one closed school staff member overheard an administrator say that the closed school should have been closed down long ago. They expressed that *"negativity"* meant teachers coming into the building did not feel *"quite welcome"* (Closed school teacher, School 5).

The fact that "us" vs. "them" dynamics surfaced in welcoming schools is consistent with existing theories and prior research that suggest that tensions and conflicts often emerge in unstable environments (such as newly integrated schools), resulting in an unequal balance of power and influence.[90] Staff and students in receiving schools had more influence because they were already embedded within the community and had a collective identity. Staff and students coming into welcoming schools from closed schools, on the other hand, had less influence and were seen as outsiders who were not yet part of the collective identify of the welcoming school. Because the district designed the process so that certain schools were closed and merged into an established welcoming school, there was a general notion that the closed community would have to assimilate into the welcoming community. This is in contrast to situations where schools go through a consolidation process in which the expectation is not one of assimilation into one of the schools, but of co-creation between two or more schools that are blended together to form a completely new school.

Closed school students also felt unwelcomed and marginalized in the welcoming schools, especially the first year of the merger. As was the case with the staff, many students coming from the closed schools also felt unwelcomed in the welcoming schools the first year of the merger. Students felt marginalized because they said welcoming school staff members spoke about them as significantly *"different"* from the students already in the welcoming schools. Similar to what happened with the staff, closed school students were labeled as the closed school students—setting them apart from the other students. In addition, closed school students in many of the instances were seen as needing more remedial academic supports and requiring far greater social-emotional and discipline-related supports than students already in the welcoming schools. This *"othering"* happened across all six schools, even when students from the closed school had prior achievement levels that were the same or higher than students in the welcoming school. In many of the cases, welcoming school staff members held negative opinions about the closed schools. As one welcoming school teacher explained, *"The opinion of a lot of the teachers was that the students who were coming over here were just going to mess up our school"* (Welcoming school teacher, School 1).

Characterizations for how closed school students would negatively affect the dynamics in welcoming

---

[90] Fligstein & McAdam (2011).

schools took many forms. For example, in four of the schools, welcoming school staff members and administrators said that students coming from the closed schools were much less academically prepared than students already in the welcoming schools, and therefore, would bring down test scores. In these schools, displaced students heard adults talking about how they were lower achieving and may have internalized the negative perceptions. For example, in one school, staff openly discussed the fact that the students coming from the closed school came in with lower test scores than the other students.

> Student 1: *"Even the teachers. Like on my first day back here, even the teachers would even say, 'Oh, you're a [closed school] kid, so you're lower than the rest of the kids, 'cause [the welcoming school was] such a high [scoring] school.'"*
> Student 2: *"And they'll [teachers] make it seem like we're not smart."* (Closed school students, School 1)

Closed and welcoming schools' student test scores were statistically significantly different in School 1, but in three of the other schools, students and staff still perceived that the closed school students were lower achieving, even when they were not, on average. Welcoming school students also talked about the closed school students as needing more remedial support. One student said, *"Some students was on different levels from you, so then they [teachers] have to reteach stuff that you already know that other people don't know. So then it would basically put you behind"* (Welcoming school student, School 2). The district promised to move closed school students from lower-rated schools into higher-rated schools, thus welcoming school perceptions were not surprising. However, this dynamic solidified the impression that closed schools served lower achieving students, even though not all closed school students were lower performing than the welcoming school students (**see Figure 2 in Chapter 1 on p.20**).

Across all six schools, welcoming school staff said that displaced students had far greater social-emotional needs, resulting in more behavior issues, than students who were already in the welcoming schools. One welcoming school teacher said when referring to students from the closed school;

"... the [closed school] students were different, if I'm being honest; like they were different." This teacher elaborated by saying that students coming from the closed school were *"out of control"* and needed more *consistent discipline support."* (Welcoming school teacher, School 5)

Another welcoming school teacher said she saw, *"an astronomical increase in kids with social problems going on at home. Kids needing to see the counselor"* (Welcoming school teacher, School 1). Others described students coming from the closed schools as having more *"emotional baggage."*

In some instances, welcoming school students perpetuated negative stereotypes of the closed school students in the first year of the merger. For example, closed school students in two different schools said that some welcoming school students called them *"savages."* In another school, staff and students talked about the closed school students as being a bad influence on the welcoming school students. As one welcoming student explained, misbehavior increased after the merger because the bad behavior of the closed school students rubbed off on the welcoming school students.

Closed school students in the six schools felt marginalized, but to what extent did the merger affect students' assessments of trust in their teachers in other welcoming and receiving schools across the district? *My Voice, My School* survey data show that students' trust in their teachers was negatively affected after the merger across all designated welcoming schools (**see Figure 5**). Students were asked questions such as whether they believed that teachers keep their promises, that they feel safe and comfortable with their teachers, and that teachers listen to students' ideas. **Figure 5** shows that students in designated welcoming schools reported lower levels of trust in their teachers after the merger than before the merger. The figure also shows that eventually, trust between students and teachers improved over time.

Tensions between closed and welcoming school staff and students occurred as a result of school culture clashes and differences in expectations. As mentioned above, when staff or students come into a new school environment, they often go through a process of socialization to learn the way things are done in the school.

FIGURE 5

Students' Assessment of Trust in their Teachers was Lower After the Merger, but Improved Over Time

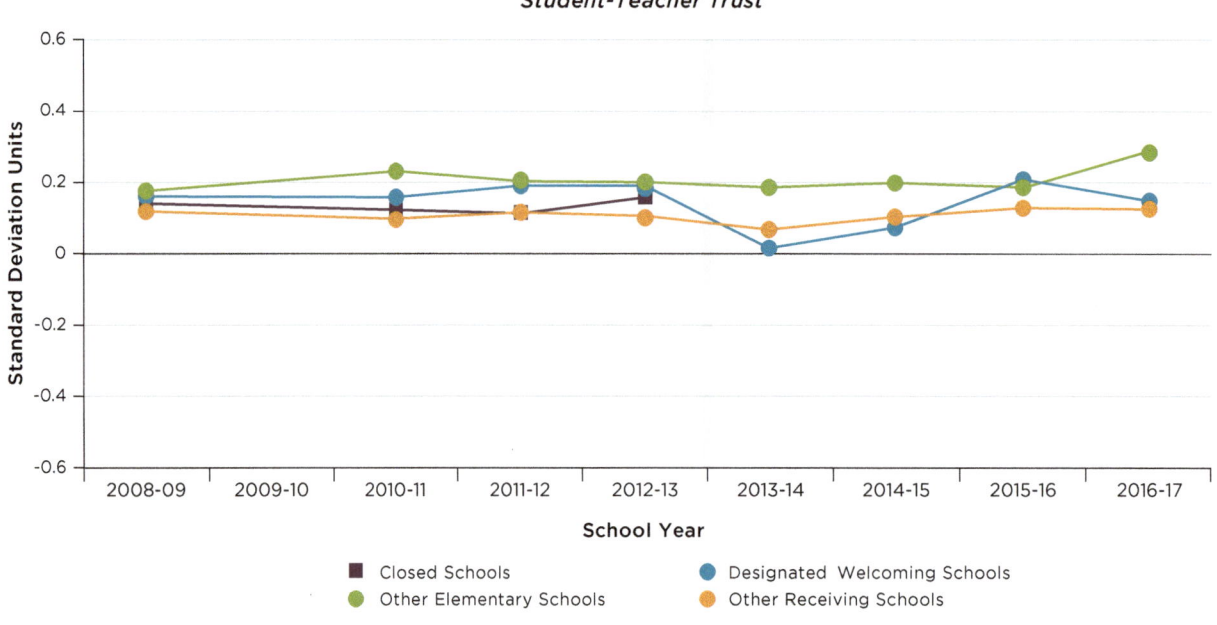

Note: This graph represents student responses on the *My Voice, My School* surveys. They reported on the school they attended in that particular year. The measure was standardized to have a mean of zero and standard deviation of one by year. A value of zero represents the average across the district. See Appendix B for more details.

One of the reasons staff tensions arose and persisted in welcoming schools that first year was because there was an expectation by the welcoming school staff that the closed school staff and students would be socialized into, conform with, and adjust to the welcoming schools' ways of doing things. For example, one welcoming school principal talked about relaying their schools' expectations to the newly joined staff:

"We actually met with [closed school teachers] in advance, during the summer ... just [so that they] know what [our school] is about and what our expectations were for how we interact with students, about integrity, our integrity, which is very important to us, about the level of instruction that we [expect]... and what has to happen in order for our students to be successful." (Principal, School 4)

The above quote illustrates how most welcoming school staff expected closed school staff to meet their expectations and embrace the culture of the receiving schools. Some staff and students coming into these schools, however, challenged the new expectations. One school counselor described the dynamics:

"... there was a little tension in the beginning with some of the teachers coming in and they're not having their principal and they're kind of having a new set of expectations. That was met with some, a little bit of angst—I'll put it like that—and some did not take it well and some decided to leave." (School counselor, School 2)

Another closed teacher said that in the welcoming school she joined, teachers were expected *"to rise to the occasion. Get in or fit in or [you're] out"* (Closed school teacher, School 4). As mentioned above, teacher and student mobility was an issue the first year of the transition. Several principals believed that students and teachers left the welcoming schools at higher rates than previous years because of the rough transition period and differences in culture and expectations.

These conflicts emerged across the six schools, but we also wanted to investigate how pervasive these dynamics were across all of the welcoming schools. *My Voice, My School* survey data showed that staff relationships across all of the designated welcoming schools declined during the year of the transition. **Figure 6** displays survey responses of teacher-teacher trust averaged across all 48

FIGURE 6

Trust Among Teachers in Designated Welcoming Schools Declined the Year of the Merger

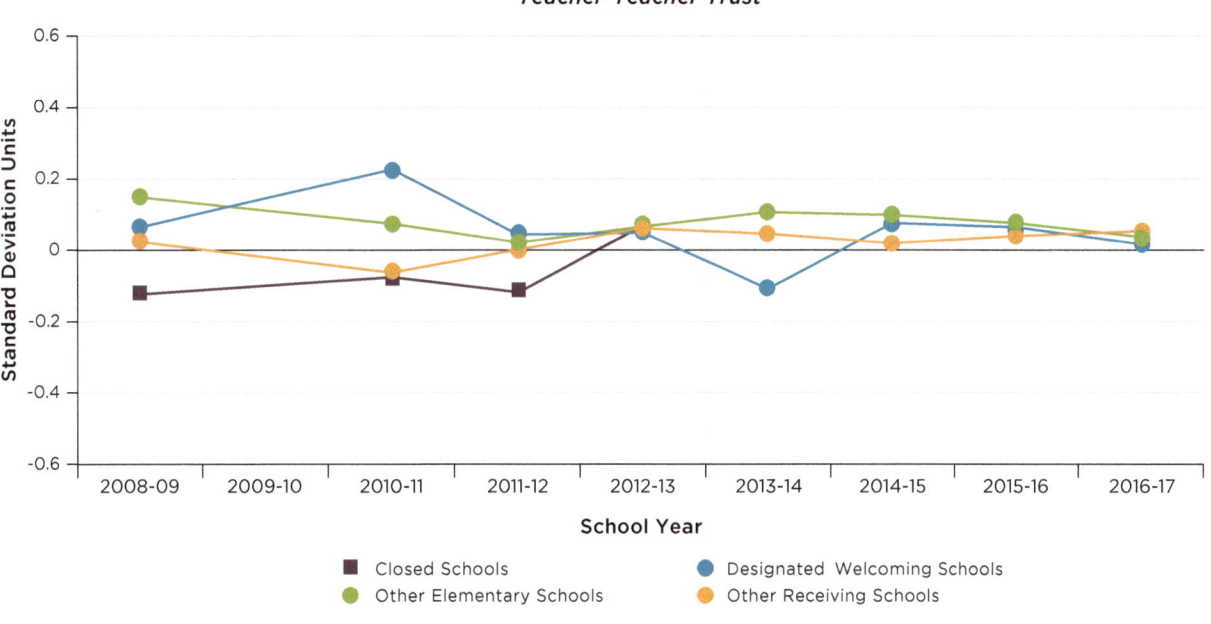

Note: This graph represents student responses on the *My Voice, My School* surveys. They reported on the school in which they worked in that particular year. The measure was standardized to have a mean of zero and standard deviation of one by year. A value of zero represents the average across the district. See Appendix B for more details.

welcoming schools from the 2008–09 school year until the 2016–17 school year. Survey items included questions such as teachers in this school trust each other, feel respected by other teachers, and feel comfortable enough to discuss feelings, worries, and frustrations with other teachers.

As shown in the figure, trust between teachers in designated welcoming schools dropped the first year of the transition (from 2012–13 to 2013–14). Trust also dropped a bit in the other receiving schools—schools across the district that took in displaced students—in the 2013-14 school year. However, by the second and third year after the merger, staff relationships appeared to have improved. It is worth noting that teacher trust in the closed schools in years prior to the announcement year was lower than other schools across the district. It was only during the announcement year that trust improved in these schools— matching the average levels of teacher trust in the district.

Over time, staff who came from closed schools and staff already in welcoming schools began to form new common identities. After the first year, relations between teachers in all six schools improved. As one closed school teacher put it, *"It is definitely not that feeling of us against them anymore"* (Closed school teacher, School 6). And another teacher said, *"Right now, I think we are more like a family, now, because after four years, it's getting better. Little by little, it's getting better"* (Closed school teacher, School 1).

There was an increase in fights and bullying between students from the closed and welcoming schools. Over time, student relationships improved. As a result of feeling marginalized in the welcoming schools, staff and students said there was an increase in student fights and bullying, especially the first year of the transition. For example, one student said, *"That's one thing that's increased a lot—fights and drama. Drama's the most major thing—"* (Welcoming school student, School 1). Welcoming school staff and students, in each school, identified students coming from the closed schools as the instigators and troublemakers. For example, one staff member from a welcoming school said students from the closed school were *"fighters."* Another teacher reiterated this sentiment, saying:

"Our school prior to being a welcoming school had discipline issues, but they were not as severe as the discipline issues that we experienced when we became a welcoming school." (Welcoming school teacher, School 6)

In other instances, closed school students were labeled as *"hostile"* or as *"rougher"* and more *"aggressive"* than welcoming school students. In most cases, staff acknowledged that closed school students were entering into the welcoming school only because they lost their school, so to many it was not surprising that they were angry. However, welcoming school staff reported that they did not have the support or training they felt they needed to handle students' grief and anger.

Across all designated welcoming schools the first year of the merger, the percentage of teachers who indicated on the *My Voice, My School* surveys that such things as physical conflicts, threats of violence toward teachers, gang activity, and general disorder increased substantially from the previous year. After that first year, teachers' perceptions of conflict within the schools decreased, but those perceptions remain higher than before the merger (**see Figure 7**). Prior to school closings, teachers in the closed schools reported the highest incidences of conflicts and threats compared to teachers in other schools across the district. Four years after the merger, the level of conflict and disorder teachers felt fell in-between the prior levels at both the receiving and closed schools.

Students across all designated welcoming schools also reported an increase in fights and bullying in their schools. **Figure 8** shows that the year of the merger, students were more likely to report having to worry about crime and violence in their schools. Students in designated welcoming schools also reported higher incidences of being bullied, teased, or threatened the year of the merger. Over time, students' reports of these incidences lessened. Nonetheless, students coming from closed schools reported much higher incidences of conflict than students in other buildings, suggesting that the social needs of these students may have been different than for other students across the district.

Staff attributed increases in student fights to a number of possible reasons. Some thought that it stemmed from long-standing rivalries between the two student populations, whereas others believed that closed school students had a hard time adjusting to the expectations of the welcoming schools and were still dealing with mourning their previous schools. Many staff believed that discipline policies tended to be lax in the closed schools, so students were not used to consequences for poor behavior. Still others believed these issues stemmed from the various social-emotional learning needs of the incoming student population, mixed with welcoming schools not being prepared to deal with these issues adequately that first year. Displaced students did say that they had a rough time adjusting because they still identified with their closed schools and felt sad that it closed. One student from a closed school agreed that their behavior got worse when they came to the welcoming school. They said,

"I argued ever since I got to [the welcoming school]. I would argue with my teachers a lot. And it's crazy because that was never a problem for me, never a problem for me at [the closed school]." (Closed school student, School 1)

Some welcoming school students from this school also felt neglected, suggesting that the staff focused so much on helping the closed school students that they *"forgot"* about the students from the welcoming school. In other schools, displaced students said they felt like they were blamed for the poor behavior of a very small group of students. Even four years following the closings, students said some of the comparisons and stereotypes lingered, but it has gotten better over the years.

Rivalries and feelings of alienation ran high during the first year of the merger, but students across all six schools said that relationships between the two student populations improved over time. Eventually students became friends with one another and no longer identified as being from the closed or welcoming schools. For example, one student said of their school now:

"I like the people that go here 'cause it's like I wouldn't say it's the same [as before the merger], but even though it took a while for everyone to get used to it, it's like we all have fun now. We joke around with each other. It's almost like a family to me." (Welcoming school student, School 1)

Another student also talked about adapting to the welcoming school, saying, *"I didn't like it [the welcoming school] at first at all but then I became more accompanied to it and I got through it"* (Closed school student, School 6). Overall, interviewees felt like the students adapted more quickly than the adults did. As one teacher put it:

FIGURE 7

Teachers' Assessment of Conflict and Disorder Increased After the Merger, Especially the First Year

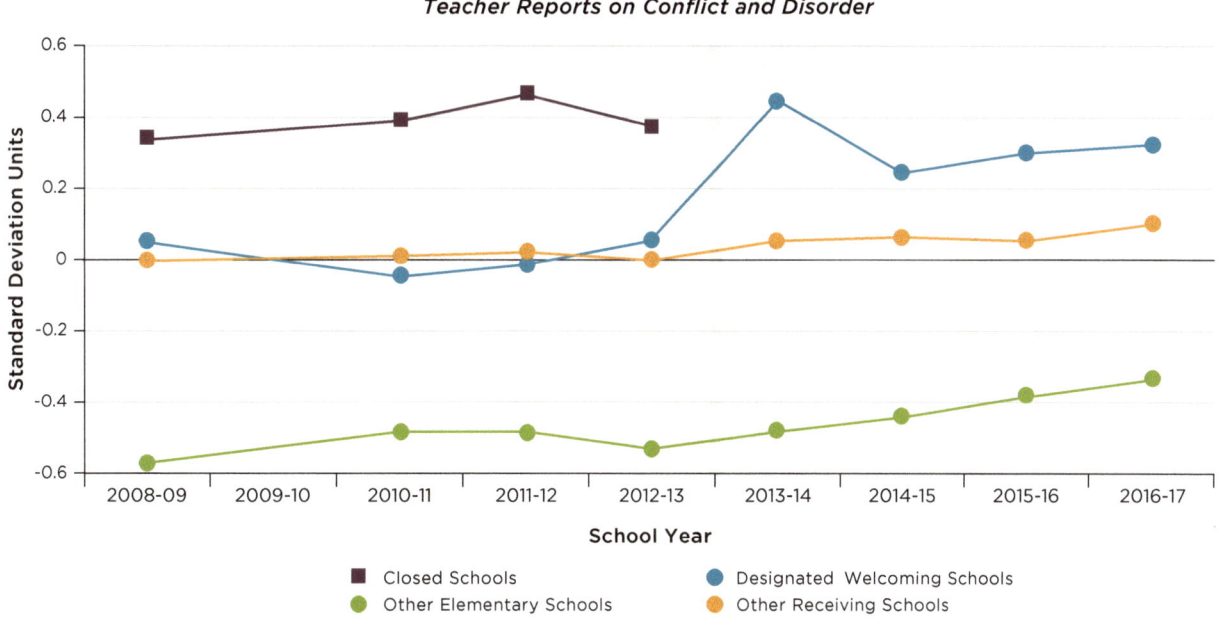

Note: This graph represents teachers responses on the *My Voice, My School* survey Teacher Safety measure. They reported on the school in which they worked in that particular year. The measure was standardized to have a mean of zero and standard deviation of one by year. A value of zero represents the average across the district. See Appendix B for more details.

FIGURE 8

Students' Assessment of Conflict and Bullying Increased After the Merger, Especially the First Year

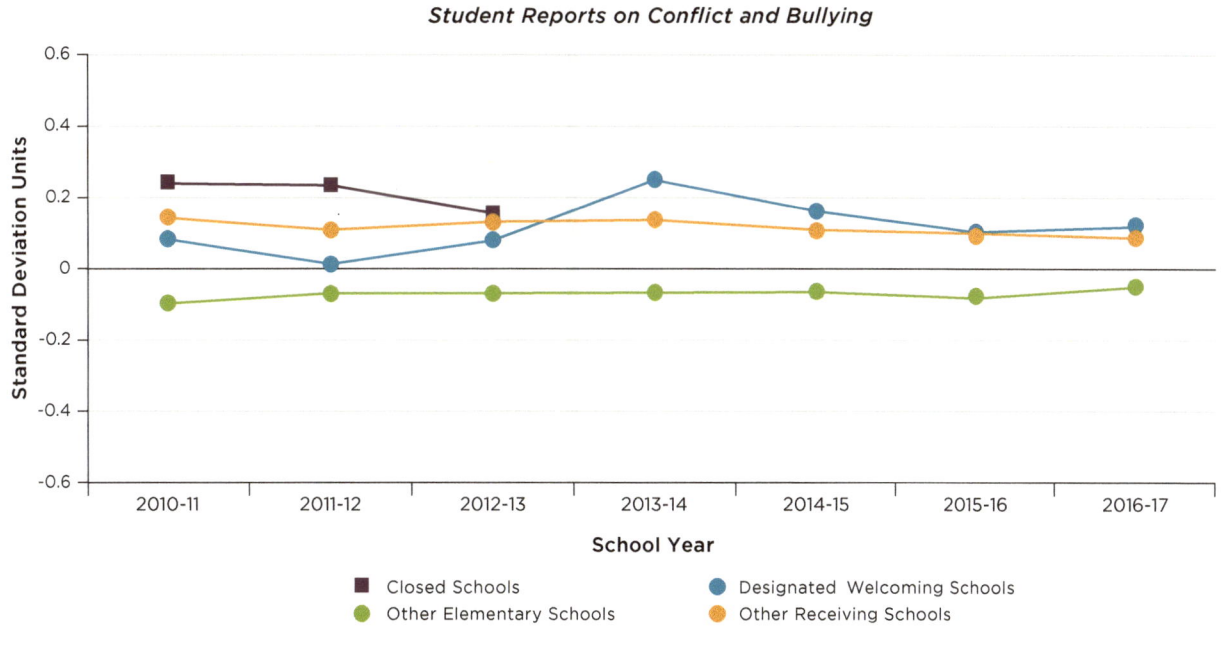

Note: This graph represents student responses on the *My Voice, My School* survey School Safety measure. Higher values on the graph represent more conflict and bullying. They reported on the school they attended in that particular year. The measure was standardized to have a mean of zero and standard deviation of one by year. A value of zero represents the average across the district. This particular measure was asked for the first time in the school year 2010-11. See Appendix B for more details.

UCHICAGO Consortium Research Report | School Closings in Chicago

"Students adapt a lot faster than adults do, so that's a good thing about being a child. I think that the students have—at the beginning, it was really difficult for them, because they felt ostracized... But, in general, I would say that the kids pretty much adapted well. By the second year, they were already building friendships, and doing that a lot. I think it was easier for the kids than it was for the adults."
(Closed school teacher, School 1)

When schools close and displaced staff and students are sent into receiving schools, it is important to recognize the complex relational dynamics at play. In all of the schools in our sample, relationships suffered and trust was lost, which affected the culture and learning environments of the schools. Prior to the actual merger, school communities felt as if they were competing with one another to stay open, which made accepting the loss and merging into the welcoming schools that much more difficult. Creating social cohesion and strong school cultures in welcoming schools took time and a great deal of support. Closed school staff and students came into welcoming schools grieving and in some cases resentful that their schools closed, while other schools stayed open. Welcoming school staff and students also grieved the way their school used to be, and educators said they were unprepared to deal with new populations and resulting divisions. Furthermore, leaders did not know what it took to be a successful welcoming school, suggesting a need for more ongoing training, reflections, and support. Staff and students said that it took a long period of time to build new school cultures and feel like a cohesive community.

In the next chapter, we widen our lens to look at the average effects of closing schools on a variety of student outcomes. We explore not only the effects on students whose schools were closed schools but also on the students already attending designated welcoming schools.

Wished-for Supports: Building Community

When asked what relational supports staff and students wished they had during the school closings process to support building relationships and community in the welcoming schools, and throughout the first years after the merger, they gave a variety of suggestions, including:

- Validation for their feelings of loss and grief. Affected staff, students, and families mourned the loss of their schools and what their schools meant for their community. They wanted that loss to be recognized by the district.
- More support, training, and guidance on how to merge schools and create a new school culture together. Newcomers entering into welcoming schools also wanted welcoming school staff to acknowledge that there are different ways of doing things.
- More thoughtful and proactive planning and training around what staff might anticipate happening when schools merge, including strategies for how to address potential divisions resulting from an "us" vs. "them" mentality.
- Support groups or other venues to voice their concerns, feelings, and needs throughout the process for all those affected, including staff, students, and families from both welcoming and closed school communities.
- More general emotional support for staff, along with an acknowledgement that the merging process was very difficult to go through. In general, staff felt like there was a great deal of focus on students, which was warranted, but not any emotional support for adults throughout the process.
- Longer-term social-emotional supports for students. Students' grief, loss, subsequent behavior, and academic needs did not end at the end of the first year of the merge. Staff said they wanted supports to last at least through the second year.
- More communication, clarity, and transparency from the district during the announcement year and closings process.

CHAPTER 4

Impact on Student Outcomes

Chapters 2 and 3 focused on the experiences of students and staff in six welcoming schools as they merged their populations with the one from the closed schools. This chapter zooms out and describes the average impact of school closings on all students affected by the 2013 closures through the 2016-17 school year. Using administrative data, we analyzed school transfer rates, number of days absent, suspension rates, reading and math test scores, and core GPA for students from closed schools, as well as students from the welcoming schools.

As described previously, the district intended for students from closed schools to transfer to higher-rated welcoming schools to improve their academic opportunities. Welcoming schools also had to have enough available seats in order to accommodate students coming from the closed schools. The district made investments in welcoming schools to expand students' learning opportunities, such as implementing a new STEM program or IB. By consolidating the school populations, welcoming schools would have more resources due to increased enrollment and extra funds associated with student-based budgeting. In theory, these efforts pointed to potential enhanced learning environments for displaced students, as well as for students in the designated welcoming schools, that could improve student outcomes.

At the same time, the challenges of merging the student and staff populations could potentially negatively affect student outcomes. Previous chapters showed that disruptions were common and trust was low in the case study schools, at least in the first year. The merger brought new challenges that could interfere with educators' ability to provide an environment conducive to learning. In addition, all the students from closed schools had to attend a new school with the added stress of adjusting to new rules, expectations, curriculum, and peers. Students already enrolled in welcoming schools also had to adjust to increased class sizes and larger schools in general. In addition, 14 of the welcoming schools moved to the closed school building, meaning that these students also faced new commutes to school and different building conditions.

We studied a range of student outcomes to offer a nuanced picture of the impacts of school closures. We started by looking at student mobility—whether displaced students changed schools again within a year—after the first transition from their closed schools. If the school attended right after the closures was not a good fit, students might have been more likely to change schools to find a better fit. Moreover, welcoming school students might have transferred out of these schools prior to the merger or in subsequent years. We also explored student absences as a measure of whether students were engaged in school and because it is a good predictor of student performance.[91] Furthermore, we examined changes in student suspension rates over time. In previous chapters, we learned that staff and students reported more fights among students after the merger and found that students were experiencing loss and stigmatization. Lastly, we explored changes in student performance. We followed students' test scores in math and reading, and core GPA, to measure the degree to which students' improved their academic performance. Core GPA is associated with a higher likelihood of being on-track in ninth grade and graduating from high school, much more than test scores, so it is an important indicator to review.[92]

We examined student outcomes over nine years: four years pre-closures (from 2008-09 to 2011-12), during the year of the announcement (2012-13), and four years post-closings (from 2013-14 to 2016-17) to show how

---

[91] Aucejo & Romano (2016).

[92] Allensworth, Gwynne, Moore, & de la Torre (2014).

the outcomes changed.[93] Our sample is comprised of students who were in grades K-7 in spring 2013, which included 10,708 students from closed schools and 13,218 students from welcoming schools.[94]

How we determined the effects of school closures on student outcomes. In order to determine the effects of school closures on student outcomes, we compared the trajectories of students affected by closures with students in similar schools that were not affected by any school actions.[95] These comparisons allowed us to estimate how students would have performed had their schools not been affected by school closures. These comparisons also helped to take into account other changes that occurred in the district that should not be attributed to the impact of school closures, such as the change to the disciplinary policy in 2013–14. The figures presented in this chapter display how much higher or lower the outcome would have been for the affected students, focusing on the effects of the policy (**see box entitled 'Measuring the Effects of School Closures' on p.47 for more details on methods and figures**). For readers interested in the outcome trends over time for affected students, **see Appendix B.**

We compared the outcomes of students from closed schools to a group of students in similar schools before the decision to close schools was final. To do this, we selected the students who were attending the other schools that were on the potential closing list in February 2013 and were not affected by any school actions, such as turnaround or being a welcoming school. These were 49 elementary schools that were not closed, but were also underutilized (their average utilization rate was 51 percent) and either rated "on probation" (Level 3) or in "good standing" (Level 2); they enrolled 14,734 students in grades K-7 in May of 2013.[96] The comparison group of students were attending similar schools to the closed ones and in the absence of closures, the displaced students would have been in similar circumstances. Thus, the outcomes of students in the comparison group serve as a way of measuring the expected outcomes for students in closed schools, had their schools not closed.

Similarly, we compared the outcomes of students from welcoming schools to a group of students that were in similar schools to the welcoming schools prior to the merger. Welcoming schools were selected to be higher-rated based on the accountability rating given to schools in 2012–13 at the time of the decision, within a mile of closed schools, and with enough seats to accommodate the students from closed schools. We selected a comparison group of schools to satisfy the same criteria, meaning they were higher-rated than the closed schools and had enough capacity to withstand a large influx of students. One small difference was that we selected comparison schools that were just beyond a mile (between 1 mile and 1.3 miles from closed schools). Because they were over a mile away, these schools were not under consideration to be welcoming schools, but they were similar to those schools in other characteristics. There were 73 comparison schools within the 1 to 1.3 mile distance satisfying these restrictions serving 25,947 students in grades K–7 in May 2013.[97] These comparison schools had an average utilization rate of 65 percent, and a similar distribution of performance levels as the welcoming schools.[98]

---

93 Because we study the outcomes of a group of students in grades K-7 in May 2013 and follow them over time, the estimated effects in the first year post-closures are based on all students since all students should be in grades 1–8 in the 2013–14 school year. However, because we looked over time, the estimated effects in later years were based on students who remained in elementary grades. For example, the students who were in fourth grade the year of the announcement were in eighth grade in 2016–17. Thus, students that were in upper grades aged-out of the sample over time.

94 See 'A Look at Student Characteristics' box on p.48 and Appendix B for details on the characteristics of the students.

95 The methodology used is commonly known as a difference-in-difference approach because it compares changes in the affected group to the changes in a comparison group. See Appendix B for more details on the statistical models and the comparison groups.

96 See 'A Look at Student Characteristics' box on p.48 and Appendix B for details on the characteristics of the students.

97 See 'A Look at Student Characteristics' box on p.48 and Appendix B for details on the characteristics of the students.

98 See Appendix B for more details on the comparison group of schools for the welcoming students.

Measuring the Effects of School Closures

To estimate the effects of closing schools on student outcomes, we used a method called difference-in-difference. This approach infers the impact of an intervention, such as school closures, by comparing the pre- to post-intervention change in the outcome of interest for the treated group relative to a comparison group. The key assumption of this method is that the comparison group should have a similar trend before intervention to the trend of the affected group. When this is satisfied, the comparison group outcomes are a credible estimate of the trends of the affected group in the absence of the intervention. By comparing the actual outcomes of the affected group by the estimated trend for this group based on the comparison group, we can estimate the effects of the intervention.

Figure A depicts the approach. The left-hand panel shows the trends of a hypothetical outcome for a group of students affected by school closures and a comparison group. In our analysis we used data from 2008–09 to 2016–17: four years pre-closures (2008–09 to 2011–12), the announcement year (2012–13), and four years post-closures (2013–14 to 2016–17). The outcome trends for both groups of students are parallel, which we tested in our statistical models in the pre-closure years. Because this assumption is satisfied, we used the post-closure trend of the comparison group to determine the possible outcome trajectory of students affected by school closures in the absence of this event (dotted line). We measured the effects of school closures by comparing the actual outcome trajectory of students affected by school closures to the predicted outcome trajectory. The right-hand panel below shows the effects of school closures—the difference between the actual and predicted outcome—on the outcome for the year of the announcement and the years post-closures. Bar graphs similar to the one below are shown in this chapter. Positive or negative effects shown in the bar graphs can happen regardless of whether the overall trends in the outcomes are improving or not. Therefore, negative effects do not indicate that overall trends are going down and positive effects do not imply that trends are going up. For readers interested in the actual outcome trends from which **Figures 9-14** were built, corresponding figures like the **line graph in Figure A are included in Appendix B.**

FIGURE A

Simulated Example of How We Estimate the Effect of School Closures on Student Outcomes

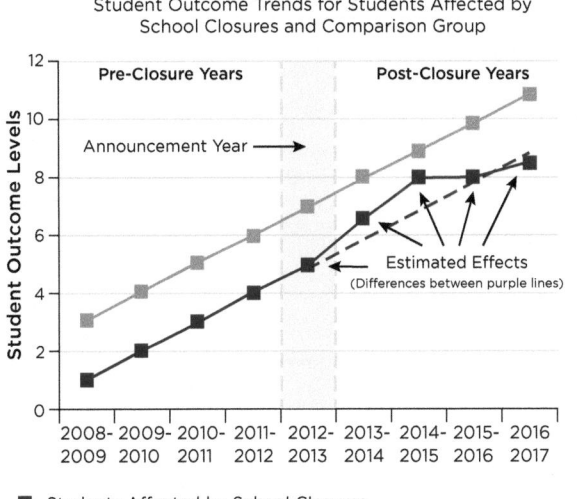
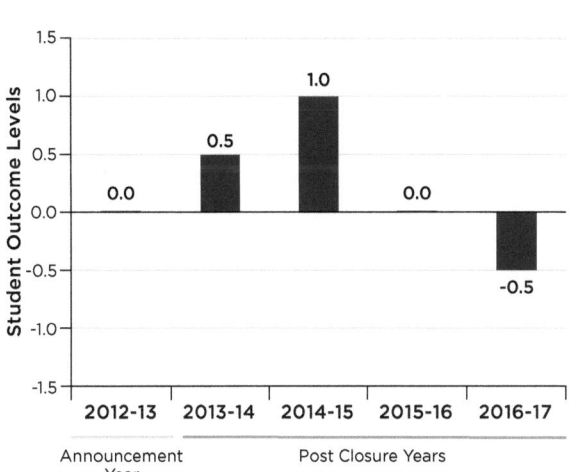

A Look at Student Characteristics

Table B shows the characteristics of students affected by closures (both from closed and welcoming schools—columns 1 and 3) and their average outcomes the year prior to the announcement. The table also contains the comparison group of students for students in closed schools (column 2) and for students in welcoming schools (column 4). For reference, the last column shows all other students in grades K–7 enrolled in other elementary schools in the district in May 2013.

The majority of students (88 percent) in the closed schools were Black students; around 10 percent were Latino. Most students (95 percent) were receiving free or reduced-price lunch and 17 percent were classified as diverse learners. Students in the comparison group shared very similar characteristics. Their outcomes prior to the announcement year were also very similar. In contrast, these two groups of students were more likely to change schools, had higher absences and suspensions, and lower test scores than other elementary school students in the district.

Three-quarters of students in the welcoming schools were Black students; one-quarter were Latino. Most students (92 percent) were also receiving free or reduced-price lunch and 15 percent were classified as diverse learners. The racial composition of students in the comparison group had a slightly higher proportion of Latino students (26 percent) and a lower proportion of Black students (66 percent). Other characteristics and outcomes were very similar between these two groups of students. On average, students in welcoming schools had lower transfer rates, absences, and suspensions, and higher test scores than students in closed schools. However, students in welcoming schools were still lagging behind other elementary school students in the district.

TABLE B

Description of Students in Grades K-7 in May 2013

Student Characteristics	1. Students in Closed Schools	2. Comparison Group for Students in Closed Schools	3. Students in Welcoming Schools	4. Comparison Group for Students in Welcoming Schools	5. All Other Students in Grades K-7
Number of Students	10,708	14,734	13,218	25,947	174,490
Black	88%	84%	74%	66%	26%
Latino	10%	13%	22%	26%	55%
Free/Reduced-Price Lunch	95%	94%	92%	90%	82%
Students with Disabilities	17%	16%	15%	14%	12%
Old for Grade	15%	15%	11%	11%	6%
Transferred School Fall 2012	23%	20%	18%	18%	13%
Number of Days Absent 2011-12	11 days	11 days	9 days	9 days	7 days
Percent Suspended 2011-12	13%	12%	7%	7%	3%
ISAT Reading Test Spring 2012*	-0.40 Standard Deviation Units	-0.40 Standard Deviation Units	-0.19 sStandard Deviation Units	-0.13 Standard Deviation Units	0.06 Standard Deviation Units
ISAT Math Test Spring 2012*	-0.45 Standard Deviation Units	-0.45 Standard Deviation Units	-0.18 Standard Deviation Units	-0.14 Standard Deviation Units	0.06 Standard Deviation Units
Core GPA** 2011-12	2.4	2.3	2.5	2.6	2.9

Note. Eighth-graders were excluded because nearly all progressed to high school the following year and thus were forced to change schools regardless of whether their elementary schools were closed or not. * Test scores were standardized to have a mean of zero and standard deviation of one using the data from the 2012-13 year in order to be able to combine the scores of students in all grades. One standard deviation unit is roughly 30 ISAT points. On average students have shown annual growth of 12 ISAT points in reading and 14 ISAT points in math. For example, students in closed schools were almost half a standard deviation below the average student in the district. That translates to 15 ISAT points, more than a year of growth behind the average student. ** Core GPA is the combination of grades from English, math, science, and social studies classes.

School transfer rates increased more than expected during the merger year for students in welcoming schools that relocated to the closed school building; no significant effect after the merger for either group of students. Not only did students from closed schools all transfer to a new school in fall 2013 due to school closings, but students in welcoming schools also left their schools for other schools at higher rates in the summer prior to the merger. In fall 2013, 21 percent of the welcoming school students did not return to these schools. This number was almost 5 percentage points higher than expected given their prior school mobility and given the mobility trends of other students in similar schools (**see Figure 9**). Although the school transfer rates for the welcoming school students remained higher than expected the next three years, those effects were not statistically significant.

As described previously, 14 of the welcoming schools had to relocate to one of the closed school buildings.[99] Because students at these 14 welcoming schools had to start a new commute and attend school at a new building, families might have decided to look for other school options. School transfer rates for these students were higher in fall 2013 (27 percent) than for students in other welcoming schools that did not have to move buildings (19 percent). The higher school transfer rates of welcoming students who had to relocate to closed school buildings drove the overall increase in school transfer rates the year of the merger (a statistically significant effect of 12 percentage points). Students in the other welcoming schools that did not move into a closed school building did not have significantly higher school transfer rates (an effect of 3 percentage points, but not statistically significant).

All students from closed schools had to transfer to other schools the year of the merger, but their school transfer rates were not affected in subsequent years after their schools closed. The estimated effects were small and not statistically significant (**see Figure 9, panel A**). The school transfer rate was around 20 percent during the years after closings for displaced

FIGURE 9

Students from Welcoming Schools were More Likely to Have Transferred Schools in Fall 2013

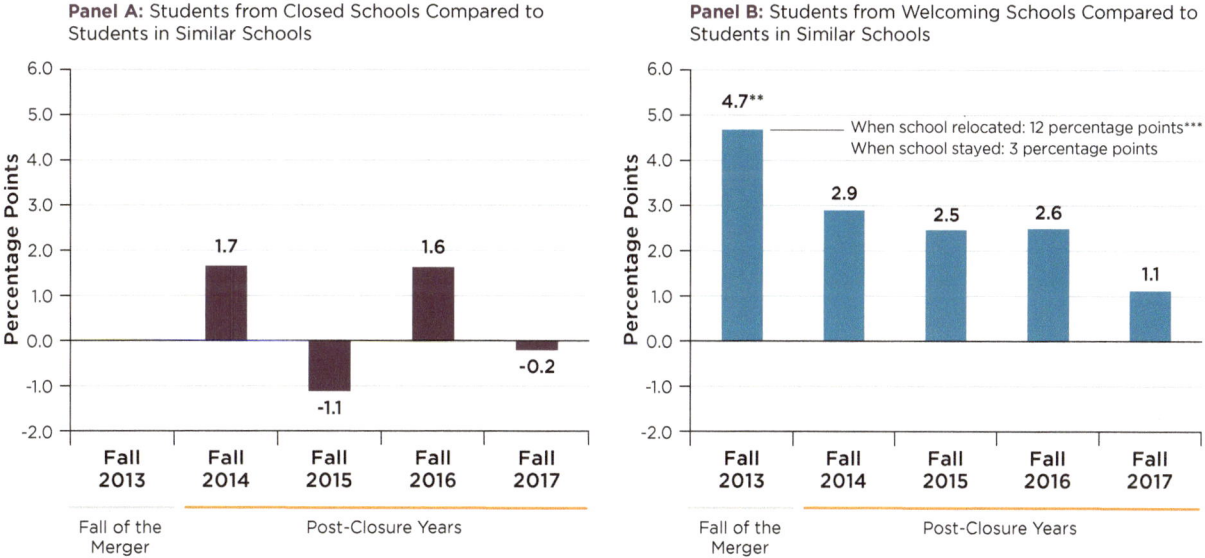

Estimated Effects of School Closures on School Transfers On:

Panel A: Students from Closed Schools Compared to Students in Similar Schools

Panel B: Students from Welcoming Schools Compared to Students in Similar Schools

When school relocated: 12 percentage points***
When school stayed: 3 percentage points

Note: This figure shows the estimates of the effects of school closures. The estimates represent how much higher or lower the outcome would have been for the affected students in the absence of the closures. The higher school transfer rates of welcoming students who had to relocate to closed school buildings drove the overall increase in school transfer rates the year of the merger (a statistically significant effect of 12 percentage points; see Panel B). These estimates come from statistical models described in Appendix B. Significance levels: *** $p<0.001$; ** $p<0.01$; * $p<0.05$.

---

[99] In some instances, the district provided transportation for the students of the welcoming schools to attend these schools.

students. In general, school transfers were decreasing for students included in the analyses. **Figure B.1 in Appendix B** displays the school transfer rates over time.

Students affected by school closures (both the closed and welcoming school students) had no changes in absences and suspension rates. Given what we learned in the six case study schools, one might have expected that the school climate would have had an effect on attendance and suspension rates overall. However, this was not the case. Absences and suspension rates showed similar trends after the merger to the trends for students in comparison schools.

Figure 10 displays the estimated effects of school closures on absences. Absences increased slightly for students in closed schools the year of the announcement (0.7 days) and one-year post-closures (0.5 days), but in general, the effects were small and statistically insignificant for both groups of students.

The average number of school days missed went up for all students in 2012–13 (**Figure B.2 in Appendix B** displays the trends over time for this outcome). It is not clear why there was an increase in absences that year, but a few things took place that might help explain part of the rise. The year was unique because the school year was extended by 10 days, and extra days were added at the end of the year to recover the time missed during the 10-day teacher strike in the fall. The slight uptick in absences, however, was a bit larger for students in closed schools and their comparison group than for students in welcoming schools and their comparison group. As communities, schools, and families were advocating for their schools not to close, this might have reduced school attendance both for students in closed schools and for students in their comparison schools, which were also on the list of potential closures.

After 2012–13, the number of school days missed by all students in our sample has been decreasing; **see Figures B.2 in Appendix B** for the trends in absences. These reductions in absences were similar for students in closed schools and their comparison group, meaning that school closures did not affect the absences of these students.

Figure 11 displays the estimated effects of school closures on suspension rates. Overall, there were no significant effects on either students from closed (**Figure 11, panel A**) or welcoming schools (**Figure 11,**

FIGURE 10

The Effect of School Closings on Absences was Small and Not Statistically Significant

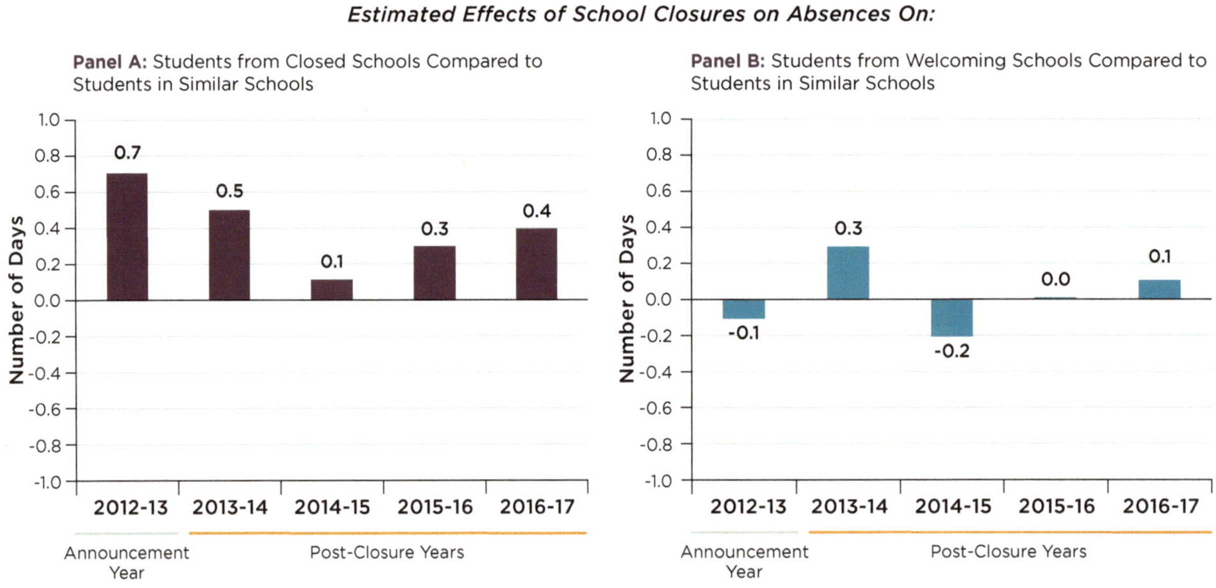

Estimated Effects of School Closures on Absences On:

Panel A: Students from Closed Schools Compared to Students in Similar Schools

Year	Number of Days
2012-13 (Announcement Year)	0.7
2013-14	0.5
2014-15	0.1
2015-16	0.3
2016-17	0.4

Panel B: Students from Welcoming Schools Compared to Students in Similar Schools

Year	Number of Days
2012-13 (Announcement Year)	-0.1
2013-14	0.3
2014-15	-0.2
2015-16	0.0
2016-17	0.1

Note: This figure shows the estimates of the effects of school closures. The estimates represent how much higher or lower the outcome would have been for the affected students in the absence of the closures. These estimates come from statistical models described in Appendix B. Significance levels: *** p<0.001; ** p<0.01; * p<0.05

panel B). Even though the effects were not significant, suspension rates were lower than expected for students from closed schools post-closure. For example, in the 2013–14 school year the suspension rates were 2.5 percentage points lower than expected given the rates of the students in the comparison group.

Suspension rates started to decline in 2013–14, which can be seen in **Figure B.3 in Appendix B**, coinciding with the change in the CPS Suspensions and Expulsions Reduction Plan (SERP). These declines were evident for all students—the ones affected by closings and the ones in the comparison groups. The declines in suspension rates for students from closed schools were slightly more pronounced than for the comparison group leading to the lower estimated effects on suspension rates presented in **Figure 11, panel A**.

We learned in Chapter 3 that students and adults in the six case studies of welcoming schools talked about an increase in disruptive behavior, but here we see that, on average, it did not translate into a larger proportion of students being suspended. The introduction of SERP in CPS encouraged schools to reduce the use of exclusionary disciplinary practices and consequently, the number of suspensions dropped districtwide.[100] In addition, suspension rates were almost double in closed schools than in welcoming schools the years before the merger (13 percent vs. 7 percent in 2011–12). Therefore, it could also be the case that welcoming school staff were used to dealing with fewer fights and other disruptive behaviors, or that their disciplinary practices were different than those in the closed schools.

Students affected by school closures experienced negative effects on test scores, especially students from closed schools. **Figure 12** shows the effects of school closures on reading and math test scores from ISAT. These tests were the state mandated tests for students in Illinois since the early 2000s. The year 2013–14 was the last time these tests were given, so we studied the effects on this test the year of the announcement and one year post-closures, and checked whether students affected by closures had similar or different pre-trends to students in comparison groups. Starting in 2012–13, CPS students began taking the NWEA tests in reading and math. Since the ISAT test was going to be retired, the district used the NWEA for

FIGURE 11
The Effect of School Closings on Suspension Rates was Small and Not Statistically Significant

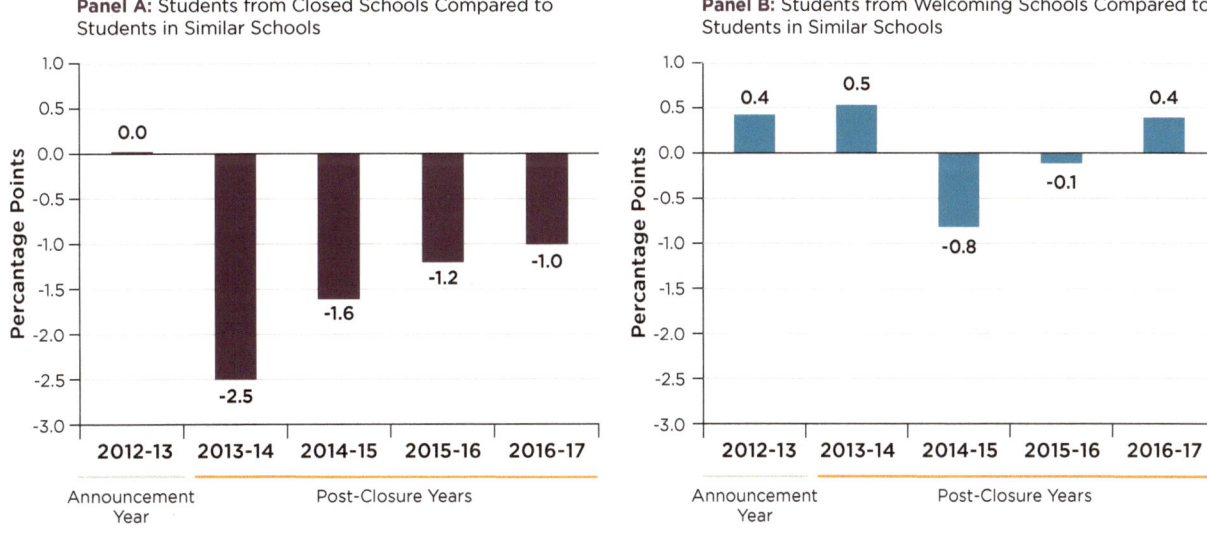

Estimated Effects of School Closures on Suspension Rates On:

Panel A: Students from Closed Schools Compared to Students in Similar Schools

Panel B: Students from Welcoming Schools Compared to Students in Similar Schools

Note: This figure shows the estimates of the effects of school closures. The estimates represent how much higher or lower the outcome would have been for the affected students in the absence of the closures. These estimates come from statistical models described in Appendix B. Significance levels: *** p<0.001; ** p<0.01; * p<0.05.

---

100 Stevens, Sartain, Allensworth, & Levenstein (2015).

FIGURE 12

Reading and Math ISAT Test Scores Were Negatively Affected the Year of, and the Year After, the Closings Announcement

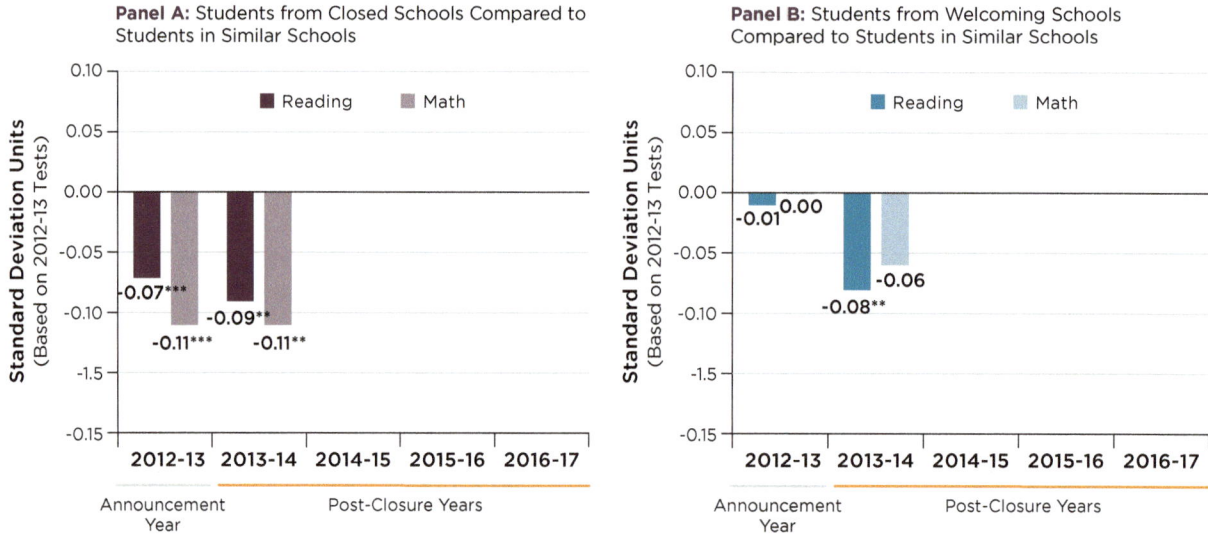

Estimated Effects of School Closures on ISAT Tests On:

Panel A: Students from Closed Schools Compared to Students in Similar Schools

Panel B: Students from Welcoming Schools Compared to Students in Similar Schools

Note: This figure shows the estimates of the effects of school closures. The estimates represent how much higher or lower the outcome would have been for the affected students in the absence of the closures. ISAT was no longer administered by CPS after the 2013-14 school year. These estimates come from statistical models described in Appendix B. Significance levels: *** $p<0.001$; ** $p<0.01$; * $p<0.05$.

---

teacher evaluation purposes and eventually for student promotion and school accountability. In 2012–13, the NWEA was mandatory in the fall (October) and spring (May), and voluntary in the winter (January). The district made the test mandatory in the winter in subsequent years. We used this test to estimate the long-term effects on test scores. **Figure 13** displays the effects on reading and math NWEA test scores. Test scores increased across the district during this time period, as shown in **Figures B.4 through B.7 in Appendix B.** However, test scores improved at a slower pace for students affected by school closings than for other students.

- **The largest negative impact of school closures was on the test scores of students from closed schools the year of the announcement.** Similar to what was found in other studies on school closures, student test scores were lower than predicted in the year of the announcement given students' prior performance. This was true for the ISAT test taken in the spring and the NWEA test taken in the spring. One reason for this might be that the announcement year was a disruptive

year for many of these schools as they faced uncertainty about whether they would be closed. Under these circumstances, the learning environment may have been affected. The district tried to avoid distractions in students' learning by waiting to announce the final list of school closures until after students took the ISAT tests. However, these students still performed lower than the comparison group, even though their performance was very similar to students in the comparison group in the pre-closure years (measured by ISAT tests) and in the fall and winter (measured by NWEA tests). Given the district's decision to wait to announce which schools they were going to close until after students took the ISAT test, it is unexpected to find a gap in test scores in March since the closed and comparison schools were under the same threat of closures at that time. Whatever the reason, students who were eventually displaced were negatively affected before they left their schools.

The negative effect was estimated to be 0.07 standard deviation units in reading in ISAT and 0.11 in math. This translated to roughly one and a half

FIGURE 13
Math NWEA Test Scores Were Negatively Affected for Students from Closed Schools, Even Four Years Later

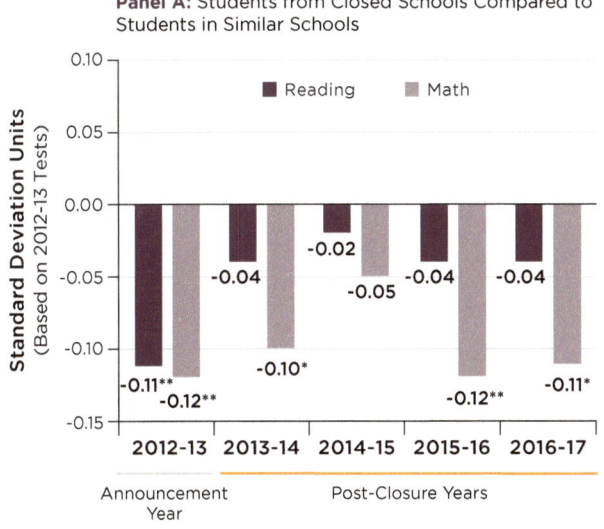
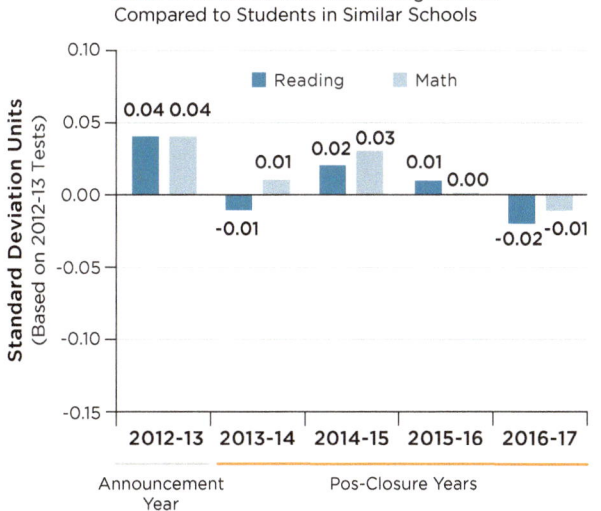

Estimated Effects of School Closures on NWEA Tests On:

Panel A: Students from Closed Schools Compared to Students in Similar Schools

Panel B: Students from Welcoming Schools Compared to Students in Similar Schools

Note: This figure shows the estimates of the effects of school closures. The estimates represent how much higher or lower the outcome would have been for the affected students in the absence of the closures. These estimates come from statistical models described in Appendix B. Significance levels: *** $p<0.001$; ** $p<0.01$; * $p<0.05$.

months behind in reading and two months behind in math.[101]

- Students from closed schools experienced a long-term negative impact on their math test scores; slightly lower, but not significant long-term effects for reading test scores. Reading test scores bounced back to their expected levels the second year post-closings for students from closed schools, but their test scores did not improve at a higher pace than students in similar schools. However, the gap in math test scores remained four years post-closings (2016–17), the last year in our analyses. This longer lasting effect in math could be driven by the fact that math learning depends upon mastering prior concepts. If key concepts were missed the year of the announcement, displaced students would have been behind their peers who were taught these concepts earlier. This lag time could explain why math test scores for displaced students were still lower than the comparison group several years later.

- Students from welcoming schools had lower than expected reading test scores the first year after the merger. Reading test scores of students from welcoming schools were negatively affected the first year post-merger by one and a half months. This was a short-term effect as the reading test scores rebounded a year after. Welcoming school students also had slightly lower than expected math scores, although this was not a significant difference. These effects may not be surprising given the disruption involved in the merger.

On average, effects on core GPA were small, although some negative effects were evident three and four years post-closures for students from closed schools. The core GPA of students from welcoming schools (**see Figure 14, panel B**) was not affected by school closures, either positively or negatively. The effects were also very small for students from closed schools (**see Figure 14, panel A**) in the first couple of years post-closures.

---

[101] These numbers were calculated knowing that one standard deviation is around 30 ISAT points and an average annual growth of 12 ISAT points for reading and 14 ISAT points for math.

FIGURE 14

Most of the Effects on School Closures on Core GPA were Negligible, Although in Later Years Core GPA was Negatively Affected for Students from Closed Schools

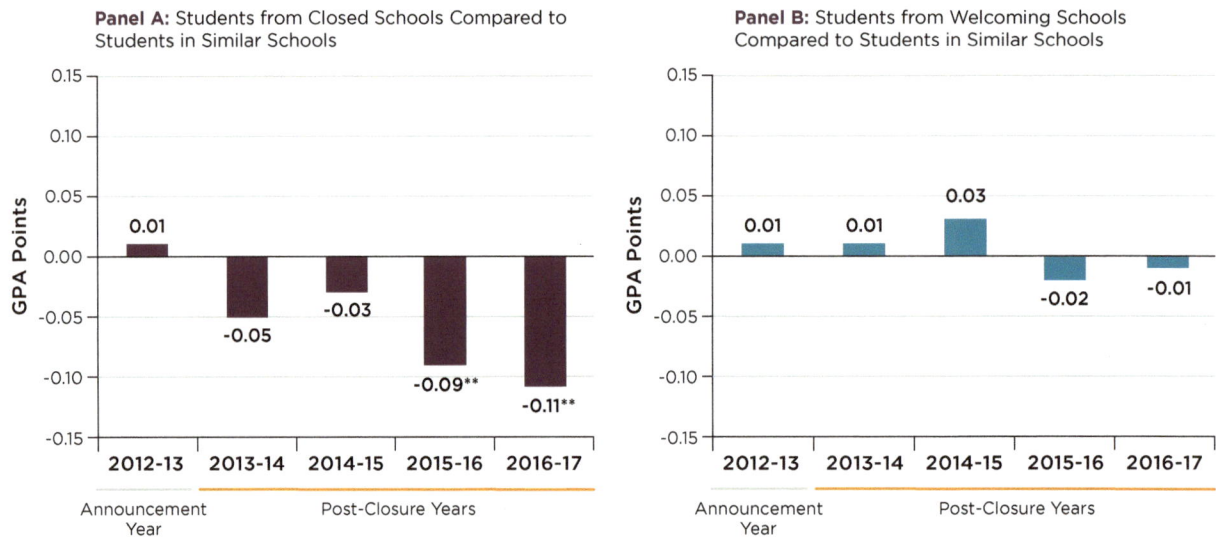

Estimated Effects of School Closures on Core GPA On:

Note: This figure shows the estimates of the effects of school closures. The estimates represent how much higher or lower the outcome would have been for the affected students in the absence of the closures. These estimates come from statistical models described in Appendix B. Significance levels: *** $p<0.001$; ** $p<0.01$; * $p<0.05$.

However, in subsequent years, displaced students' core GPA was lower than expected by 0.1 GPA points. These effects were estimated only by considering students' core GPA while in elementary schools. Recall that given the way the sample was selected, these negative effects in the third and fourth years post-closures were based on students who were affected by closures while they were in earlier grades. For example, students who were in eighth grade in 2016–17 were most likely in fourth grade the year of the announcement. It is students in grades 3–5 that account for the negative effect in the later years—when they were in middle grades (**see Figure 15**). In other words, groups of students were affected differently, with the effects on GPA driven primarily by younger students who were displaced; the negative GPA effects for these students manifested once they were in middle school.

It is worth noting that core GPA has been increasing slightly over time for the affected students, especially the years after school closures. This can be seen in **Figure B.8 in Appendix B.** Thus, while students from closed schools had lower core GPAs than expected, their GPAs followed district-wide trends and improved over time. In addition, while the increase in core GPA was similar for students from welcoming schools and their comparison group, there is a slight gap for students from closed schools and their comparison group in the last years (**shown in Figure 14**). On average, the core GPA of students from closed schools was lower than the core GPA for students from welcoming schools prior to the announcement. It was still lower post-closings despite the positive trend in core GPA.

Many students were affected by the school closures in 2013. Students in 47 elementary schools had to continue their elementary years at a different elementary school. Students and staff in 48 welcoming schools had to get ready to receive these students, an average of 150 per school. Fourteen of these welcoming schools had to move to the building of the closed school and adapt to a new setting. In many cases displaced students attended schools with peers who, on average, were absent fewer days, less likely to be suspended, and higher performing. The merger of these student populations, and the staff as well, was challenging, perhaps making these environments, at least initially, less conducive to learning and student engagement.

FIGURE 15
Negative Effects on Core GPA Were More Pronounced Three Years Post-Closings for Students in Grades 3-5 in 2012-13

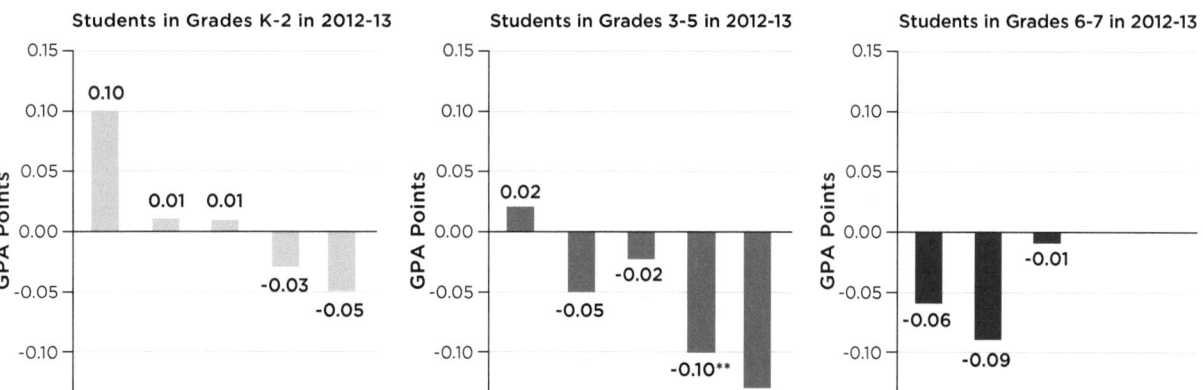

Estimated Effects of School Closures on Core GPA by Students' Grades in 2012-13 On Students from Closed Schools Compared to Students in Similar Schools

Note: This figure shows the estimates of the effects of school closures. The estimates represent how much higher or lower the outcome would have been for the affected students in the absence of the closures. These estimates come from statistical models described in Appendix B. Significance levels: *** p<0.001; ** p<0.01; * p<0.05.

We asked whether student outcomes were affected by the 2013 school closings. We learned that not only students from closed schools were affected, but also students from welcoming schools. Most of the effects on welcoming students were short-lived. School closures led to higher mobility for students in the 14 schools that moved buildings. It also led to lower reading scores than expected the first year of the merger. Other outcomes we studied were not affected either positively or negatively.

The effects on students from closed schools were concentrated in their GPA and test scores, but not attendance or suspensions. These negative effects started the year of the announcement, before students even moved to a new elementary school and, at least for math test scores, continued four years post-closure. Students need more support during the year of the announcement and that support should continue not only the year of the merger, but for most of the students' elementary school career. Students affected by closures during the earlier grades were still dealing with lower than expected performance throughout their elementary school years.

CHAPTER 5

Interpretive Summary

School districts across the nation are facing enormous economic challenges and many, like Chicago, are simultaneously experiencing steep enrollment declines. Cash-strapped districts in these circumstances face tough decisions: how does a school district reduce costs, but continue to provide students with high-quality educational experiences? In 2013, Chicago officials argued that the only option they had was to "right size" the district by closing an unprecedented number of schools all at once.

Policymakers assumed that their decision to close schools would alleviate some of the financial burden and align resources where they were needed most. They also believed that by consolidating resources, students would have greater access to programs, supports, and services that they did not have in their former schools. District officials hoped that students transferring to higher-rated welcoming schools would experience improved academic outcomes. As then-CPS CEO Barbara Byrd-Bennett promised, although closing schools would not be easy, "I also know that in the end this will benefit our children." [102]

While rationales for closing schools may appear straightforward to policymakers, justifications are often unconvincing for those most directly affected. Fierce resistance often arises because it is the community that must bear the burden of going through the closing process. Community members worried about a number of potentially negative consequences, including community destabilization, increases in violence, and students ending up in poor learning environments. Opponents also decried the fact that these closings mainly affected families and students living in historically disinvested, primarily Black areas of the city.

Our main research question, then, was: Did closing schools provide students with better educational opportunities and stronger academic outcomes? The evidence provided in this report suggests that closing schools and moving students into designated welcoming schools to consolidate resources did not automatically expose them to better learning environments and result in greater academic gains. At the same time, many of the negative concerns that critics raised did not materialize. A number of different factors played a role in why students did not benefit as much as hoped and why it was difficult for leaders and staff to create positive and welcoming learning environments, especially the first year of the merger.

As districts across the country grapple with the decision to close schools, this report offers some evidence that the intended benefits of closing schools may not materialize. In particular, we offer the following points for consideration:

Schools slated for closure need support the year of the announcement. In the majority of studies done on school closures thus far, including this one, students experienced a slowdown in their achievement trajectories the year of the announcement. This suggests that the announcement itself interrupts the learning environment in schools slated for closure. It is possible, we speculate, that because staff and students in Chicago

---

[102] Chicago Public Schools. (2013, March 21b)

spent time and energy fighting to keep their schools open, it may have influenced the learning climate in their schools. It is also possible that once the decision was made, students and staff—who were mourning the loss of their schools—were not able to focus as much on teaching and learning. Staff, students, and families in these circumstances need much more support, starting the year of the announcement, to help potentially mitigate the learning loss.

The lengthy decision period during the 2012–13 school year heightened anxiety, anger, and distrustfulness felt in the affected communities. The magnitude of closing so many schools amplified the disruption. Having schools essentially compete to stay open over an extended period resulted in feelings that there were "winners" and "losers," and caused fractures in some communities who would then be expected to work together. Furthermore, it limited the window for school leaders and staff to plan and prepare adequately for the transition into welcoming schools

Inadequate preparation of the learning environment can aggravate feelings of loss. Leaders in welcoming schools wanted to provide students, staff, and their families with an updated, clean, and inviting learning space. This requires sufficient time, and strong organization and planning for moving supplies and preparing buildings. It also requires thinking beyond the technical aspects of the move to consider the more adaptive elements that emerge when accommodating such large influxes of staff and students. School leaders need support in thinking about and planning for how a change of this magnitude will affect the day-to-day school operations, social interactions, and general functioning of the school. Although the district planned for upgrades and other logistical considerations, the monumental task of moving approximately 95 school buildings in a matter of months required much more time and considerably more resources than was provided. This is critical because preparing the physical space took valuable staff time away from building relationships and integrating communities. The physical environment affects the learning environment, so it is important to ensure that environments are welcoming; otherwise these logistical problems amplify feelings of loss. It is vital for policymakers to make sure that after closing schools, welcoming schools have all of the valued equipment and technology from the closed school, teachers have their own materials, and all staff have what they need to help support students at the beginning of the school year. After students and staff lose their schools, they should have the option to enter into receiving school buildings that feel nicer and have more resources than the schools they lost.

District leaders invested in extra professional development and additional resources to put towards extra student supports in the first year after the closures. Students and staff appreciated the extra resources, technology, programs, and the expansion of Safe Passage, although they wished for a longer-term investment because student needs did not end after one year. If the school environment is prepared adequately to receive students on time, then educators can focus on relationship building and instructional planning.

There is a need for active relationship building that acknowledges both loss and opportunity. Leaders in welcoming schools wanted to create positive and welcoming learning environments for all staff and students. But communities affected by school closures first need their grief and loss acknowledged and validated, and need more social-emotional support. The way that the closings process was set up—that certain schools would be closed and others would stay open to welcome the displaced students and staff—appeared to promote assimilation into welcoming schools, rather than co-creation of culture together. Preventing an "us" vs."them" mentality requires ongoing proactive efforts by district and school leaders. District and school leaders, for example, could work to proactively bust myths and stereotypes that staff, students, and communities have about one another. It is also important to pay attention to symbolic representations of separation (such as labeling), and instead focus on creating and promoting commonalities. In order to do this, staff and students from the closed and welcoming school communities must work together to co-create new school cultures and identities. It takes time and support to cultivate and rebuild relationships in welcoming schools and in the community at-large.

Furthermore, many of the supports were directly aimed at students with an assumption that students would be most impacted by closures. However, educators said they believed that students adapted much faster than the adults. This suggests that adults going through a closure and merging process need much more proactive support and guidance than were provided. As some interviewees expressed, becoming a welcoming school could be a positive experience, given adequate resources and support, and with a focus on co-creating new communities together.

Closing schools—even poorly performing ones—does not improve the outcomes of displaced students, on average. Closing underutilized schools was intended to enhance students' educational experiences by allowing them an opportunity to learn in a better environment. In this and other previous studies on the effects of school closures, we have seen that academic outcomes, on average, do not improve after students' schools were closed. Studies that find positive effects on displaced students only happened in cases with fewer disruptions, such as phase-outs, or when students attended top-performing schools. The affected schools included in this study closed immediately and the majority of students did not attend top-performing schools.[103] At the same time, student performance on average did not go down as much as some feared. Educators in this situation struggled, but worked hard to make it work, despite the challenges with the transition.

Students in earlier grades whose schools closed ended up earning lower than expected grades in their classes even four years later. One possible explanation for this might be that displaced students were identified as coming from lower-performing schools. This label of being from a lower-performing school may have potentially influenced how students saw themselves and ultimately impacted their long-term outcomes. Research on noncognitive factors points to the importance of students' mindsets about themselves as learners because mindsets have a powerful influence on academic performance.[104] This suggests that educators could be more proactive in trying to prevent negative academic labeling (e.g., "low performer") and focus on developing students' academic mindsets.

Closing schools can also have some short-term negative impacts, on average, for the students in receiving schools. Most of the discussions regarding the potential impacts of closing schools focus on the students in schools slated for closure, with very little attention paid to what might happen to students already in designated welcoming schools. This policy affected welcoming students in a number of ways. Relatively more students in welcoming schools transferred to other schools the year of the merger (2013–14), especially in cases where welcoming school buildings relocated into closed school buildings. This suggests that families in these circumstances also had to send their children into different neighborhoods. For students who stayed in their welcoming schools, they too faced challenges in having to rebuild their school cultures and adjust to new peers, expectations, and, in some cases, new administration. The average test scores for students in welcoming schools dropped a bit, especially in reading, but recovered over time. These findings suggest that policymakers need to think of the unique needs of students and families attending schools that welcome students from closed schools into their communities.

Five years later, the CPS budget is still tight, enrollments are still declining, the moratorium on school closings has ended, and the Chicago Board of Education has recently voted to close and consolidate more schools. School closures in Chicago, and elsewhere, are still happening in communities beset by historical disinvestment and inequities, further amplifying destabilization effects. We continue to have an equity issue: many students are not being offered the same kinds of opportunities afforded to students in higher-income, higher-resourced communities. These patterns are deeply interwoven with the historical, racial, and geographical segregation in Chicago.[105] Students across the city deserve to have access to programs, supports, and opportunities that help them learn, grow, and reach

---

103 Twenty-one percent of displaced students attended a Level 1 or "excellent standing" school. See de la Torre et al. (2015).

104 Farrington et al. (2012).
105 For more about this history, see Ewing (forthcoming).

their full potential. More must be done to address these stark inequalities. Closing under-enrolled schools may seem like a viable solution to policymakers who seek to address fiscal deficits and declining enrollment, but our findings show that closing schools caused large disruptions without clear benefits for students.

More research is needed to understand what happens to staff and students in school buildings slated for closure the year of the announcement to help unpack why we see negative effects starting in that year. In addition, we highlighted the average effects of closing schools on a variety of student outcomes, but we know that there was a great deal of variation across schools.[106] More research is needed to explore this variation and to unpack the factors that might help explain these differences. Few studies have looked at the potentially differential effects of closing schools on sub-groups of students (e.g. students with special learning needs). It is also important to investigate whether or not future generations of students benefit from attending consolidated schools. There are still lingering questions regarding the potential financial savings of consolidating buildings, and a thorough cost-benefit analysis could help address these questions. Furthermore, not much is known about the impact of closing schools on the teacher workforce.

The decision to close schools is never an easy one, nor is it clear-cut. By looking at a wider array of outcomes and by including the experiences and voices of the people directly impacted by school closures, we can develop a more holistic understanding of the effects of school closures. Our hope is that this report will add to our collective understanding of the effects of school closings.

---

106 For example, there was variation in the proportion of closed school staff and students who joined welcoming schools, in the performance level of the welcoming/receiving schools, as well as how different closed schools were from the welcoming/receiving schools in terms of their performance.

Commentary

Eve L. Ewing
Provost's Postdoctoral Scholar
School of Social Service Administration
at the University of Chicago

"All they [the district] did was put in air conditioners ... But they were dragging their feet, and the building wasn't clean. And I really think that was a systemic issue."

These words, spoken by a principal at a designated welcoming school, illustrate the importance of this insightful and necessary report on the 2013 closure of 50 Chicago Public Schools. Building on their prior research on the topic, the authors have compiled a study that makes clear two things that should inform future proposed school closure decisions: the paramount importance of the notion of "respect" as part of any such process, and the ecological reality of the context within which such decisions are made.

"They Just Don't Care:" The Question of Respect in School Closure Processes

In several places throughout the report, teachers and staff expressed feeling a lack of respect on the part of the school district, which left them with negative sentiments in the wake of school closures. School personnel experienced the move from one building to another as disorganized and chaotic, and viewed the loss or destruction of valuable school materials as a sign of disrespect. "CPS doesn't care. They just don't care, and it shows." Other principals described arriving in buildings with bathrooms that lacked doors or stall locks, corridors that were half-painted, and facilities that were "filthy."

In these cases, respondents said explicitly that they felt a lack of planning reflected a lack of respect. But the theme of respect is implicit in other areas of the findings. For instance, participants indicated that after a period of time the transition plan paperwork they filled out became less about creating a useful document, and more about complying with the requirement.

In other words, the transition plan was not worthy of their respect, and the necessity of completing it did not reflect respect on the part of the district (as opposed to, say, being able to create and modify a dynamic plan as unanticipated factors arose over time).

Earlier studies have found that those impacted by school closures felt disrespected by the process leading up to the closure.[107] This report reveals that this theme of respect remains salient even as the receiving schools transition into the task of uniting two disparate school communities. Why does respect matter? Because of the interwoven and longitudinal nature of relationships, both within schools, and between schools and district leaders. The 2013 school closures certainly do not represent the last time district leaders will require compliance with a large-scale policy action. Indeed, as of this writing, CPS has been recently entangled in another round of highly visible and highly contentious school closures. Each time these occasions arise—whether they be school closures, new graduation requirements, new application and attendance guidelines, or any other broad-scale actions—the district asks, essentially, for trust and faith from the stakeholders it serves. And each time the district is perceived as disrespectful in its actions, the cache of such trust and faith erodes a bit further. Given that CPS lost approximately 10,000 students[108] last year, it is safe to say that trust is not a commodity we can spare.

An Ecological View on School Closure Decisions

This report's focus on the dialectic relationship between receiving schools and closing schools represents a significant contribution to the literature. As the methodological approach implies, the profile of a prototypical receiving school and prototypical closed

---

[107] Ewing (2016); Lipman, P., Vaughan, K., & Gutierrez, R.R. (2014). *Root shock: Parents' perspectives on school closings in Chicago.* Chicago, IL: Collaborative for Equity & Justice in Education.

[108] Perez, J. (2017, October 20). Chicago Public Schools enrollment drops by nearly 10,000 students. *Chicago Tribune.* Retrieved from http://www.chicagotribune.com/news/local/breaking/ct-met-chicago-schools-population-drop-20171020-story.html

school were actually quite similar, thanks in part to the constraints needed to designate a school as a "welcoming school." Since designated "welcoming schools" needed to be within one mile of a closing school and Chicago is racially and socio-economically segregated, the two types of schools were largely demographically similar. And since receiving schools required adequate space to handle an influx of students, many of them had also been on the initial proposed schools list. Perhaps most notably, many students and teachers at so-called "welcoming schools" also experienced loss as they had to relocate from a familiar building into an unfamiliar building, and they saw higher-than-expected rates of mobility from their classmates and teachers.

In other words, perhaps we should no longer think about the impact of closures in terms of "closed schools" and "receiving schools" as two distinct entities, and even less as "losers and winners." Rather, we should understand that all of these schools exist within an ecological matrix that created barriers to them optimally functioning as sites of excellent instruction. Though their challenges may differ, these schools are all struggling under the weight of closures—past closures, threatened closure, nearby closures, actual closures, responding to closures—and the possibility that they might very soon be on the proverbial chopping block once again.

Thus, the findings contained in this report suggest that an ecological view of school closures would be more helpful—a view that understands each student, each teacher, and each school as situated within a dynamic ecosystem alongside other schools, the neighborhood in which they are located, and the broader social context of Chicago and its present and historical struggles.[109]

Within this framework, the extraordinary stress and even harm caused by the nature of the pre-closure process is cast into relief. All schools involved in the closure process—whether in schools that would ultimately be closed or that received students—were embroiled in a highly stressful, internally competitive, even antagonistic process that established their institutional futures as being threatened by the institutional survival of their colleagues and neighbors. Given this context—which one participant in this study refers to depressingly as resembling "the Hunger Games"—any social cohesion that schools were able to develop whatsoever post-closure should be seen as nothing short of miraculous.

Ultimately, as the authors' conclusion suggests, we must ask how and why we continue to close schools in a manner that causes "large disruptions without clear benefits for students." Taken together, these two insights—the importance of respect and the ecological nature of school closures' effects—suggest that the calculus regarding school closure is much more complicated and difficult to anticipate than perhaps the district was prepared for. Determining costs and benefits goes beyond the already-complex measures of student academic achievement, building capacity, and financial costs. Rather, in order to fully assess the impact a proposed school closure has on students, teachers, and communities, it is necessary to incorporate less-tangible factors, which may in fact be impossible to fully predict.

---

[109] Bronfenbrenner, U. (1977). Toward an experimental ecology of human development. *American Psychologist, 32*(7), 513-531; Johnson, G.M. (1994). An ecological framework for conceptualizing educational risk. *Urban Education, 29*(1), 34-49.

Commentary

Douglas N. Harris
Professor of Economics
Schleider Foundation Chair in Public Education
Director of the Education Research Alliance for New Orleans
Tulane University

School closings represent one of the most difficult and important issues facing all kinds of school systems today. Enrollment cycles mean that some share of school districts will always be shrinking, requiring fewer buildings. Even for districts that remain at the same size, funding per student can drop or remain stagnant, creating financial distress. Closing schools is sometimes a necessary evil.

Yet, at least in the short run, closures create challenges for students, parents, and educators, all of whom have to find new schools. Students often end up travelling farther to school and have to adjust to new school environments and make new friends. The best schools are like families and changing families is hard. School closings also mean removing community anchors. For these reasons, closing and taking over schools is arguably the last thing any school district or system leader ever wants to do.

On the other hand, some recent research suggests that the effects of closure are not quite what they seem. If the lowest-performing schools are closed, then students end up in better schools. Despite the initial disruption, even the students in schools at the time of their closure end up better off in the long run. Moreover, future generations of students benefit from having a better menu of schools to choose from.

This is what we found in New Orleans, where the state aggressively closed low-performing schools and replaced them with new charter operators starting around 2014. System leaders closed the lowest-performing schools—lowest in terms of achievement growth—and, two years later, elementary students were doing better than we would have predicted if they had stayed in their old schools. Better schools, better results.

This important new report from the UChicago Consortium presents a different picture. Not only did students from closed schools experience a short-term decline in achievement, but this persisted for several years afterwards. They did not bounce back. It is entirely unclear why we see results different from New Orleans, but one possible reason is that the schools that were closed in Chicago were not those with the lowest achievement growth. When we focus on outcome levels, whether they be test scores or attendance, we end up attributing to schools what is actually due to factors outside school control.

Another possibility is that when one school is closed, even the remaining schools are affected. The Consortium report illustrates that nearby schools that remain open face an influx of students (and educators) from the closed schools. To address these challenges, the leaders of Chicago Public Schools identified specific "welcoming schools" near the closed schools that would receive support for making the difficult transition.

Through interviews with educators in welcoming schools, this Consortium report shows that the adjustment was difficult. Planning was poor and the additional supports provided to schools were mostly temporary. Even the seemingly basic step of physically moving equipment and supplies was carried out too slowly and the welcoming schools were not ready at the beginning of the school year. The best-laid plans are not meaningful without effective implementation.

While this report addresses elementary schools, Chicago is now in the process of phasing out a number of high schools. Looking across cities, the effects of closure are clearly more negative in these higher grades. In our study of school closure and takeover in New Orleans, we found that students in closed high schools were less likely to graduate high school and attend college because of the closures. This pattern—one that we have seen when looking across cities—is most likely because high school students have less time to adjust and meet the academic requirements for graduation. Making friends is also more difficult for teenagers when moved to new social environments, leaving students more isolated. Elementary school students, in contrast, are almost automatically promoted to the next grade, have more time to bounce back and benefit from better schools, and have an easier time making new friends.

Given the problems with the city's last round of closures in 2013, and the even greater challenges that await high schools, Chicago Public Schools may be in for even greater problems ahead. Even if they do choose the truly lowest-performing schools, the district has an obligation to plan better and provide even more resources to schools in this next round of closures. One option to consider, and one used in New Orleans, is to give students in closed schools priority to choose any school they wish. High school students are willing and able to travel farther to school, and this may allow them to find a school that is a better fit. The receiving schools should also consider making special accommodations to get students into the courses they need. Assigning extra counselors to help students make the adjustment is another option.

This Consortium report provides a valuable service to the people, and especially the students, of Chicago. It also adds to the growing body of evidence nationally, which points to several key conclusions and recommendations: First, school closure should be a rare occurrence. When it is done, it is essential that system leaders focus on closing the schools that are truly lowest-performing—something most state-mandated school ratings are ill-designed for. System leaders should also do what they can to eliminate the short-term pain for students and educators. The dictum that we should "do no harm" is especially appropriate. We must pay attention to the short-term effects of education decisions on current students, even as leaders try to create a system of schools designed to serve future generations.

References

Agreement between the Board of Education of the City of Chicago and Chicago Teachers Union Local 1, American Federation of Teachers, AFL-CIO. (2012, October 24)
Retrieved from https://www.ctunet.com/for-members/text/CTU_Contract_As_Printed_2012_2015.pdf

Ahmed-Ullah, N.S. (2013, April 25)
At Chicago school closing hearings, crowds fade. *Chicago Tribune.* Retrieved from http://articles.chicagotribune.com/2013-04-25/news/ct-met-cps-closing-hearings-20130426_1_schools-chief-barbara-byrd-bennett-final-list-two-community-meetings

Allensworth, E., & Easton, J.Q. (2007)
What matters for staying on-track and graduating in Chicago Public Schools. Chicago, IL: University of Chicago Consortium on Chicago School Research.

Allensworth, E.M., Gwynne, J.A., Moore, P., & de la Torre, M. (2014)
Looking forward to high school and college: Middle grade indicators of readiness in Chicago Public Schools. Chicago, IL: University of Chicago Consortium on Chicago School Research.

Anderson, C.L. (2014)
The disparate impact of shuttered schools. *American University Journal of Gender, Social Policy & Law, 23*(2), 319-351.

Arcia, E. (2007)
A comparison of elementary/K-8 and middle schools' suspension rates. *Urban Education, 42*(5), 456-469.

Aucejo, E.M., & Romano, T.F. (2016)
Assessing the effect of school days and absences on test score performance. *Economics of Education Review, 55,* 70-87.

Banchero, S. (2010, January 17)
Daley school plan fails to make grade. *Chicago Tribune.* Retrieved from http://articles.chicagotribune.com/2010-01-17/news/1001160276_1_charter-schools-chicago-reform-urban-education

Barrow, L., Park, K., & Schanzenbach, D.W. (2011)
Assessing the impacts on students of closing persistently failing schools (Working Paper).

Belsha, K., & Kiefer, M. (2017, February 12)
Empty schools, empty promises: What happened to the closed school in your neighborhood? *The Chicago Reporter.* Retrieved from http://chicagoreporter.com/what-happened-to-the-closed-school-in-your-neighborhood/

Branham, D. (2004)
The wise man builds his house upon the rock: the effects of inadequate school building infrastructure on student attendance. *Social Science Quarterly, 85*(5), 1112-1128.

Bross, W., Harris, D.N., & Liu, L. (2016)
The effects of performance-based school closure and charter takeover on student performance. New Orleans, LA: Tulane University: Education Research Alliance for New Orleans.

Brummet, Q. (2014)
The effects of school closings on student achievement. *Journal of Public Economics, 119,* 108-124.

Bryk, A.S., Sebring, P.B., Allensworth, E., Luppescu, S., & Easton, J.Q. (2010)
Organizing schools for improvement: Lessons from Chicago. Chicago, IL: University of Chicago Press.

Byrne, J., & Ruthhart, B. (2013, May 22)
School closings disappoint many alderman. *Chicago Tribune.* Retrieved from http://www.chicagotribune.com/news/local/breaking/chi-school-closings-disappoint-many-aldermen-20130522-story.html

Catalyst Chicago. (2007, December 1)
Map: Still waiting for better schools. Retrieved from http://www.chicagoreporter.com/map-still-waiting-better-schools/

Chicago Housing Authority. (n.d.)
Plan for transformation. Retrieved from http://www.thecha.org/about/plan-for-transformation/

Chicago Metropolitan Agency for Planning. (2017a)
Demographic shifts: Planning for a diverse region. Retrieved from http://www.cmap.illinois.gov/documents/10180/475314/FY17-0054%20Demographics%2Snapshot/8a9caead-a16a-4cba-a57d-7ffcbf33a1c0

Chicago Metropolitan Agency for Planning. (2017b)
Socioeconomic shifts in the Chicago region. Retrieved from http://www.cmap.illinois.gov/updates/all/-/asset_publisher/UIMfSLnFfMB6/content/socioeconomic-shifts-in-the-chicago-region

Chicago Public Schools. (n.d.)
Chicago Public Schools fiscal year 2014. Retrieved from http://cps.edu/finance/FY14Budget/Pages/schoolsandnetworks.aspx

Chicago Public Schools. (n.d.)
Facility standards. Retrieved from http://cps.edu/About_CPS/Policies_and_guidelines/Pages/facilitystandards.aspx

Chicago Public Schools. (n.d.)
Parents. Retrieved from http://www.cps.edu/qualityschools/Pages/parents.aspx

Chicago Public Schools. (n.d.)
Renaissance 2010. Retrieved from http://www.cps.edu/PROGRAMS/DISTRICTINITIATIVES/Pages/Renaissance2010.aspx

Chicago Public Schools. (2012)
2012-13 Guidelines for school actions. Retrieved from http://www.cps.edu/ABOUT_CPS/POLICIES_AND_GUIDELINES/Pages/2013GuidelinesforSchoolActions.aspx

Chicago Public Schools. (2012, November 2)
CPS CEO Barbara Byrd-Bennett to launch thorough community engagement process on school actions. Retrieved from http://cps.edu/News/Press_releases/Pages/11_02_2012_PR1.aspx

Chicago Public Schools. (2013, January 10)
Statement from CEO Barbara Byrd-Bennett on release of commission on school utilization report. Retrieved from http://cps.edu/News/Press_releases/Pages/01_10_2013_PR1.aspx

Chicago Public Schools. (2013, February 13)
Based on community feedback, CPS releases detailed criteria to help guide decisions on district's utilization crisis. Retrieved from http://cps.edu/News/Press_releases/Pages/2_13_2013_PR1.aspx

Chicago Public Schools. (2013, March 20)
CPS CEO Byrd-Bennett unveils supports for students in all welcoming schools. Retrieved from http://cps.edu/News/Press_releases/Pages/3_20_2013_PR1.aspx

Chicago Public Schools. (2013, March 21a)
Media briefing. Retrieved from https://cbschicago.files.wordpress.com/2013/03/cps-briefing.pdf

Chicago Public Schools. (2013, March 21b)
Significant new investments to provide quality, 21st century education for CPS students transitioning from underutilized schools this fall. Retrieved from http://cps.edu/News/Press_releases/Pages/3_21_2013_PR2.aspx

Chicago Public Schools. (2013, August 22)
Special curriculum to address students' emotional needs. Retrieved from http://cps.edu/Spotlight/Pages/spotlight466.aspx

Cole, M., & Cole, S. (1993)
The development of children (2nd Ed.). New York, NY: Scientific American Books.

Commission on School Utilization. (2013)
Final report. Chicago, IL: Commission on School Utilization.

Cook, P.J., MacCoun, R., Muschkin, C., & Vigdor, J. (2008)
The negative impacts of starting middle school in sixth grade. *Journal of Policy Analysis and Management, 27*(1), 104-121.

Creswell, J.W., & Clark, V.L.P. (2018)
Designing and conducting mixed methods research (3rd Ed.) Los Angeles, CA: Sage Publications.

Deeds, V., & Pattillo, M. (2015)
Organizational "failure" and institutional pluralism: A case study of an urban school closure. *Urban Education, 50*(4), 474-504.

de la Torre, M., & Gwynne, J. (2009)
When schools close: Effects on displaced students in Chicago Public Schools. Chicago, IL: University of Chicago Consortium on Chicago School Research.

de la Torre, M., Gordon, M.F., Moore, P., Cowhy, J.R., Jagešić, S., & Huynh, M.H. (2015)
School closings in Chicago: Understanding families' choices and constraints for new school enrollment. Chicago, IL: University of Chicago Consortium on Chicago School Research.

Dowdall, E., & Warner, S. (2013, February 11)
Shuttered public schools: The struggle to bring old buildings new life. Philadelphia, PA: The Pew Charitable Trusts.

Dumke, M., Chase, B., Novak, T., & Fusco, C. (2016, June 25)
Daley's CHA plan jolted region. *The Better Government Association.* Retrieved from https://www.bettergov.org/news/daleys-cha-plan-jolted-region

Durán-Narucki, V. (2008)
School building condition, school attendance, and academic achievement in New York City public schools: A mediation model. *Journal of Environmental Psychology, 28*(3), 278-286.

Eads, D., & Salinas, H. (2014, December 23)
Demolished: The end of Chicago's public housing. *National Public Ratio.* Retrieved from https://apps.npr.org/lookat-this/posts/publichousing/

Eccles, J.S., Lord, S., & Midgley, C. (1991)
What are we doing to early adolescents? The impact of educational contexts on early adolescents. *American Journal of Education, 99*(4), 521- 542.

Engberg, J., Gill, B., Zamarro, G., & Zimmer, R. (2012)
Closing schools in a shrinking district: Do student outcomes depend on which schools are closed? *Journal of Urban Economics, 71*(2), 189-203.

Evans, G.W., Yoo, M.J., & Sipple, J. (2010)
The ecological context of student achievement: School building quality effects are exacerbated by high levels of student mobility. *Journal of Environmental Psychology, 30*(2), 239-244.

Ewing, E.L. (2016)
Shuttered schools in the Black metropolis: Race, history, and discourse on Chicago's south side (Unpublished doctoral dissertation). Harvard University, Cambridge, MA.

Ewing, E.L. (forthcoming)
Ghosts in the Schoolyard: Racism and School Closings on Chicago's South Side. Chicago, IL: University of Chicago Press.

Farrington, C.A., Roderick, M., Allensworth, E., Nagaoka, J., Keyes, T.S., Johnson, D.W., & Beechum, N.O. (2012)
Teaching adolescents to become learners: The role of noncognitive factors in shaping school performance: A critical literature review. Chicago, IL: University of Chicago Consortium on Chicago School Research.

Fink, L.L. (2010)
A comparison of grade configuration on urban sixth to eighth grade students' outcomes in regular and special education (Unpublished doctoral dissertation). University of Maryland, College Park, MD.

Firestone, W.A., & Louis, K.S. (1999)
Schools as cultures. In J. Murphy & K.S. Louis (Eds.). *Handbook of research on educational administration* (pp. 297-322). San Francisco, CA: Jossey-Bass.

Fligstein, N., & McAdam, D. (2011)
Toward a general theory of strategic action fields. *Sociological Theory, 29*(1), 1-26.

Frey, W.H. (2018, March 26)
US population disperses to suburbs, exurbs, rural areas, and "middle of the country" metros. *Brookings Institution.* Retrieved from https://www.brookings.edu/blog/the-avenue/2018/03/26/us-population-disperses-to-suburbs-exurbs-rural-areas-and-middle-of-the-country-metros/

Goddard, R.D., Tschannen-Moran, M., & Hoy, W.K. (2001)
A multilevel examination of the distribution and effects of teacher trust in students and parents in urban elementary schools. *The Elementary School Journal, 102*(1), 3-17.

Goerge, R., Dilts, J., Yang, D.H., Wasserman, M., & Clary, A. (2007)
Chicago children and youth 1990-2010: Changing population trends and their implications for services. Chicago, IL: Chapin Hall Center for Children.

Gonzalez, R., & Komisarow, S. (2017)
Community monitoring and crime: Evidence from Chicago's Safe Passage program (Working Paper). Retrieved from https://drive.google.com/file/d/0B8yV-hmMmDh7X-3prbmRXTm95bFE/view

Gutman, L.M., & Midgely, C. (2000)
The role of protective factors in supporting the academic achievement of poor African American students during the middle school transition. *Journal of Youth and Adolescence, 29*(2), 223-249.

Hirsch, A.R. (2009)
Making the second ghetto: Race and housing in Chicago 1940-1960. Chicago, IL: University of Chicago Press.

Karp, S. (2013, May, 15)
For the record: Class sizes, closing schools. *Catalyst Chicago.* Retrieved from http://www.chicagoreporter.com/record-class-sizes-closing-schools/

Karp, S. (2013, October 7)
'Structured out' of a job. *Catalyst Chicago.* Retrieved from http://www.chicagoreporter.com/structured-out-job/

Kemple, J. (2015)
High school closures in New York City: Impacts on students' academic outcomes, attendance, and mobility. New York, NY: The Research Alliance for New York City Schools.

Kirshner, B., Gaertner, M., & Pozzoboni, K. (2010)
Tracing transitions: The effect of high school closure on displaced students. *Educational Evaluation and Policy Analysis, 32*(3), 407-429.

Larsen, M.F. (2014)
Does closing schools close doors? The effect of high school closings on achievement and attainment. New Orleans, LA: Tulane University.

Lipman, P., & Haines, N. (2007)
From accountability to privatization and African American exclusion: Chicago's "Renaissance 2010." *Educational Policy, 21*(3), 471-502.

Manzo, L.C. (2003)
Beyond house and haven: Toward a revisioning of emotional relationships with places. *Journal of Environmental Psychology, 23*(1), 47-61.

McMillan, D.W., & Chavis, D.M. (1986)
Sense of community: A definition and theory. *Journal of Community Psychology, 14*(1), 6-23.

McMillen, D., Sarmiento-Barbieri, I., & Singh, R. (2017)
More eyes on the street reduce crime? Evidence from Chicago's Safe Passage Program (Working Paper). Urbana, IL: University of Illinois at Urbana-Champaign.

Merriam, S.B. (1998)
Qualitative research and case study applications in education. San Francisco, CA: Jossey-Bass.

Miles, M.B., & Huberman, A.M. (1994)
Qualitative data analysis: An expanded sourcebook. Beverly Hills, CA: Sage Publications.

Nuamah, S.A. (2017)
The paradox of educational attitudes: Racial differences in public opinion on school closure. *Journal of Urban Affairs,* 1-17.

Osterman, K.F. (2000)
Students' need for belonging in the school community. *Review of Educational Research, 70*(3), 323-367.

Papay, J.P., & Kraft, M.A. (2017)
Developing workplaces where teachers stay, improve, and succeed. In E. Quintero (Ed.), *The social side of education reform* (pp. 1-3). Cambridge, MA: Harvard Education Press.

Patton, M.Q. (2002)
Qualitative research & evaluation methods (3rd Ed.). Thousand Oaks, CA: Sage Publications.

Pettit, B. (2004)
Moving and children's social connections: Neighborhood context and the consequences of moving for low-income families. *Sociological Forum, 19*(2), 285-311.

Scannell, L., & Gifford, R. (2010)
Defining place attachment: A tripartite organizing framework. *Journal of Environmental Psychology, 30*(1), 1-10.

Schein, E.H. (1996)
Culture: The missing concept in organization studies. *Administrative Science Quarterly, 41*(2), 229-240.

Seidman, E., Allen, L., Aber, J.L., Mitchell, C., & Feinman, J. (1994)
The impact of school transitions on the self-system and perceived social context of poor urban youth. *Child Development, 65*(2), 507-522.

Simmons, R.G., & Blyth, D.A. (1987)
Moving into adolescence: The impact of pubertal change and school context. New York, NY: Aldine de Gruyter.

Starr, J.P. (2016)
The 48th annual Phi Delta Kappa/Gallup Poll of the public's attitudes toward the public schools: Why school? Americans speak out on education goals, standards, priorities, and funding. *Phi Delta Kappan, 98*(1), K1-K32.

South, S.J., & Haynie, D.L. (2004)
Friendship networks of mobile adolescents. *Social Forces, 83*(1), 315-350.

Steinberg, M.P., Scull, J., & MacDonald, J.M. (2015, February 28)
School closure and student relocation: Evidence from the school district of Philadelphia. Paper presented at the Association for Education Finance and Policy 40th Annual Conference, Washington, DC.

Stevens, W.D., Sartain, L., Allensworth, E.M., & Levenstein, R. (2015)
Discipline practices in Chicago schools: Trends in the use of suspensions and arrests. Chicago, IL: University of Chicago Consortium on Chicago School Research

Tarter, C.J., & Hoy, W.K. (2004)
A systems approach to quality in elementary schools: A theoretical and empirical analysis. *Journal of Educational Administration, 42*(5), 539-554.

Temple, J.A., & Reynolds, A.J. (1999)
School mobility and achievement: Longitudinal findings from an urban cohort. *Journal of School Psychology, 37*(4), 355-377.

Van Leeuwen, E., Van Knippenberg, D., & Ellemers, N. (2003)
Continuing and changing group identities: The effects of merging on social identification and ingroup bias. *Personality and Social Psychology Bulletin, 29*(6), 679-690.

Vevea, B., Lutton, L., & Karp, S. (2013, January 15)
The history of school closings in Chicago 2002-2012. *WBEZ.* Retrieved from https://www.wbez.org/shows/wbez-news/the-history-of-school-closings-in-chicago-200212/cdfc0755-27b9-48de-b5be-bce992124048

Weiss, C.C., & Kipnes, L. (2006)
Middle school effects: A comparison of middle grades students in middle schools and K-8 schools. *American Journal of Education, 112*(2), 239-272.

Witten, K., McCreanor, T., Kearns, R., & Ramasubramanian, L. (2001)
The impacts of a school closure on neighborhood social cohesion: Narratives from Invercargill, New Zealand. *Health & Place, 7*(4), 307-317.

Yaccino, S., & Rich, M. (2013, March 21)
Chicago says it will close 54 public schools. *New York Times.* Retrieved from http://www.nytimes.com/2013/03/22/education/chicago-says-it-will-close-54-public-schools.html

Yin, R.K. (1994)
Case study research: Design and methods (Applied Social Research Methods Series, 5). London, UK: Sage Publications.

Appendix A
Qualitative Data, Sample, and Methods

Case Study Design

The aim of the qualitative portion of the study was to gain knowledge about contexts, situations, and experiences lived by those directly affected by the school closings. In order to do this, we used a comparative case study design.[110] Case studies are examinations of bounded systems where researchers focus on the processes in context.[111] Multiple case study designs are more robust than single case designs,[112] therefore, we sampled six receiving schools to better understand the variation between welcoming schools.

Each welcoming school case was unique, so it was important to capture the experiences and school organizational environments by doing fieldwork. We found some differences in regards to transition processes and the ways in which each welcoming school integrated students and staff from closed schools, as well as accommodated existing students and staff. In addition, the composition of the teacher workforce, and the demographics and numbers of students who were welcomed into each of these schools, varied. However, we found more similarities than differences across the six case schools, suggesting that these schools experienced many of the same kinds of challenges.

Sample: Case Study Schools

The sample for the cases was both purposive and intensive.[113] The pool of schools from which we chose consisted of the 48 district-designated welcoming schools that were assigned to take in students and staff from the 47 elementary schools that closed in June 2013. Though more than 300 schools received students from the closed schools, only the schools that the district assigned to welcome students were considered. We did so because the district dedicated substantial time and resources into the welcoming schools and encouraged families to enroll their children into them.

Intensity sampling and sampling for range involves prior exploratory work to determine the nature of the variation in outcomes and contexts in order to select information-rich cases. Quantitative student outcome data and teacher and student survey data were used to identify cases. Our sampling criteria for welcoming schools included these parameters:

- **Large influx of students.** Receiving schools had to have at least 15 percent of their student population the year after closings (2013–14) come from the closed school in order to be considered. This was to ensure that the schools in our sample received a sizeable number of students.

- **Consistent administrator.** The welcoming school had to have the same administrator since the year the school became a welcoming school (the 2013–14 school year). This was critical, because we wanted to make sure that we could speak with school leaders who could answer questions about the transition to becoming a welcoming school.

- **Variation on student outcomes on standardized test scores.** Our sample had to have a range of schools with different student achievement outcomes, as measured by their math standardized test scores. We sampled schools where students were performing as expected, lower than expected, and higher than expected on their math standardized test scores, controlling for a variety of student characteristics, including prior achievement, special education status, whether or not a student was old for their grade, and socioeconomic status.

---

110 Merriam (1998); Yin (1994); Creswell & Clark (2018).
111 Creswell & Clark (2018); Merriam (1998).
112 Yin (1994).
113 Merriam (1998); Patton (2002).

- **Variation on school climate indicators.** We sampled for range on a variety of school climate indicators, including students' self-reported perceptions of safety, peer relationships, and student-teacher trust from the *My Voice, My School* surveys. We sampled two schools that were performing better than we would expect across a number of school climate measures; two schools that were not performing as well as we would expect, given the students they serve; and two schools that were scoring higher than we would expect in some school climate measures and lower than we would expect in others.
- **Geographic range.** The majority of school closings occurred in the city's south and west sides, and we chose schools in these areas. We also wanted schools from different networks, so we intentionally chose schools located in different neighborhoods and networks. Four networks and five Chicago neighborhoods are represented within our sample.

Though unintentional, our sample varied in other aspects, including on the CPS school rating the school had the year of the announcement and whether or not the welcoming school relocated into the closed school building. Two of the schools in our sample were Level 1 ("excellent standing"), one was Level 2 ("good standing") and three were Level 3 ("on probation") schools; three of the schools in our sample re-located to the closed school building.

Sample: Interview and Focus Group Participants

In order for a school to serve as a case study school, the principal at that school had to agree to both participate in an interview and to assign a staff liaison or contact person to help our research team with recruiting and scheduling interview and focus group participants. At each school, we sought to speak with:

- At least one administrator
- At least one counselor or student support staff who came from either the closed or welcoming school
- Two teachers who came from the closed school
- Two teachers who were at the welcoming school since the year of the announcement
- One focus group of seventh- and eighth-grade students from the closed school
- One focus group of seventh- and eighth-grade students from the welcoming school

All interviews and focus groups took place from March–June 2016 and were recorded and transcribed verbatim. We found there to be advantages and disadvantages to the fact that interviews took place three years after the merger. One disadvantage was that people's perspectives may have changed over time, meaning we were unable to capture their initial thoughts and feelings while they were going through the transition. At the same time, one advantage was that because interviewees were not immediately living through the change, the time delay allowed them to have some distance and clarity regarding their experiences.

In the interviews and focus groups, we asked a number of questions about the school transition period, including how leaders tackled planning for the merger, and what kinds of initial supports were offered and provided. In addition, we asked about changes in the needs of students and staff, whether and what kinds of welcoming events or training/supports were offered to staff and students. Furthermore, we asked a number of questions about changes in the teaching and learning environment in the schools, including changes in academic and other after-school program offerings, curriculum, instruction, technology, discipline, safety, and general school climate. Lastly, we asked about their overall opinions of the impact of closing schools on individuals and on the welcoming school as a whole.

Interviews with teachers typically occurred during their lunch or "prep" period and lasted approximately 45–50 minutes. Interviews with student support personnel and administrators typically lasted between 45–60 minutes. Our contact person also identified students who came from the closed and welcoming schools to participate in focus groups. They also distributed and collected signed parent permission forms for students to participate in focus groups. All student focus groups lasted about 45–50 minutes, or about one class period.

At each school, we spoke with between five and eight staff members. In one instance, we were unable to complete an interview with a principal. The principal gave permission for the school to participate and also personally agreed to participate in this study, but was unavailable on the day of our site visit. We attempted to reschedule the interview but were unsuccessful. In all five of the other cases, we spoke with the principal and in two cases, we also spoke with an assistant principal. Additionally, in every case, we spoke with four teachers (two from the closed school and two from the welcoming school) and one student support staff. Collectively, we interviewed 40 staff members.

In total, we conducted 12 student focus groups comprised of 52 students: 24 who attended closed schools and 28 who attended welcoming schools in 2012–13. In all case study schools, we were able to talk to students who had attended the welcoming school before it became a welcoming school; however, there was one case where we were only able to speak with one student who had attended a closed school, which was not the closed school that was assigned to the welcoming school. In all other instances, we were able to speak with more than one student. With the exception of the one student interview, our focus groups ranged from three to eight students, with an average of four students per focus group. In some cases where we quoted interviewees in this report, we did not reveal which school the participant came from so as to ensure confidentiality.

In addition, we also collected and analyzed school transition plans that were created by staff from each welcoming school in summer 2013.

Analysis

The case study interviews and documents were analyzed following Miles and Huberman's analytic approach: 1) We used descriptive coding to describe and summarize segments of data; 2) Next, we used pattern coding for emergent themes, relationships, explanations, and inferential analysis.[114] We first employed descriptive coding and assigned codes based on the research questions and themes that cut across the interviews, including themes from prior literature on transitions, relationships, policies and practices. Next, we employed a deeper and more inductive pattern coding using broader theories on place attachment theory, and general organizational and school culture theories as a guide. During this phase of coding, we looked for emergent themes and explanations for why interviewees experienced the transition and welcoming school environments in specific ways. We looked for patterns and themes both within each of these broader descriptive codes, but also within schools and across our sites for cross-case comparison. We then wrote case memos for each of the schools, summarizing information across interviewees by each theme. We then created cross-case matrices with information summarizing themes across all six sites. Next, we grouped our pattern codes into summaries and created a cognitive map of the similarities and differences across our cases. In addition to coding and mapping the data, researchers also produced analytic memos, which derived and developed general themes from each individual case study school.

---

[114] Miles & Huberman (1994).

Appendix B
Quantitative Data, Sample, and Methods

Data Sources and Variables

The data used for this report comes from CPS administrative records (including information on student demographics, enrollment, test scores, absences and suspensions, as well as personnel characteristics), and surveys about students' and teachers' school experiences (see **Tables B.1 and B.2**). All of these data sources are linked together using a unique student identifier.

Analysis to Select Schools for Qualitative Analyses

To identify welcoming schools that performed higher, lower, or as expected in different outcomes, we used 2-level hierarchical models (HLM) with observations over time nested within schools. The data included pre-intervention years (from 2008–09 to 2012–13) and two years post-intervention (2013–14 and 2014–15). All schools that were opened and remained opened during these years were included in the analyses. At level one, we controlled for gender, race, socioeconomic status, prior academic achievement as measured on prior math test, whether a student was receiving special education services, and whether a student was old for grade. Variables were group-mean centered around the school means across all years. All slopes were held constant across schools.

We used residual files from our HLM analysis to calculate whether schools were better than expected on each outcome. Schools were identified as performing higher than expected if the results of dividing empirical Bayes residuals by the square root of the posterior variance were greater than 1.96. Similarly, schools were identified as performing lower than expected if the results of dividing empirical Bayes residuals by the square root of the posterior variance were lower than -1.96. If the result was between 1.96 and -1.96 then schools were classified as performing as expected.

Analysis to Estimate School Closure Effects on Student Outcomes

Description of Sample

Table B.3 shows the 47 closed schools and their designated welcoming school or schools. The second column shows the utilization rates of these schools based on the fall 2012 enrollment. Utilization rates are based on the ratio of the number of students enrolled in a school compared to the ideal capacity of the school calculated by CPS. The last column represents the performance level of the schools in the year 2012-13, the year of the announcement. The performance level was assigned to a school based on ISAT test data and attendance. Schools earned points for all metrics and an index was calculated (the percentage numbers in parenthesis in the last column). Based on that index, schools were assigned one of three ratings: Level 1 ("excellent standing") schools received at least 71 percent of available points; Level 2 ("good standing") schools received between 50 and 70.9 percent of available points; and Level 3 ("on probation") schools received fewer than 50 percent of available points. Welcoming schools were selected to be higher-rated than the closed schools based on the 2012-13 performance policy rating. In cases where the rating was the same, the district paired closed schools with welcoming schools that were higher-rated on the majority of the performance policy metrics.

We identified CPS students who were enrolled in kindergarten through seventh grade as of May 2013, the date nearest to the closing announcement that our data would allow. Eighth-graders were excluded because nearly all progressed to high school the following year and thus were forced to change schools regardless of whether their elementary schools were closed or not. We then aggregated administrative data for these students dating back to the 2008-09 school year and through the 2016-17 school year, resulting in an unbalanced panel.

TABLE B.1

Description of Variables

Student Variables	Demographic variables such as gender, race/ethnicity, special education status, limited English proficiency, old for grade (suggesting the student has been retained).
Teacher Variables	Demographic variables such as gender, race/ethnicity, years in CPS, education degree and school where they were employed.
School Transfers	Among active students in the fall, how many are enrolled in a different school compared to the fall of prior year. If the student's grade in fall is not served in the school he/she was enrolled in the prior fall, then the move is considered a forced move and the student is not part of the analyses.
Absences	Annualized number of days absent. From 2008-09 to 2011-12 the number of school days were 170 days; in 2012-13 180 days, in 2013-14 178 days; and 180 days the subsequent years in our sample. Since the distribution of absences tend to be skewed, when modelling this outcome we take the natural logarithm.
Suspensions	A dummy variable taking a value of 1 if a student received an in- or out-of-school suspension during the school year; 0 otherwise.
Test Scores	Student performance on the Illinois Standards Achievement Test (ISAT) in reading and math and the NWEA test in reading and math. Scores are standardized within grade based on the 2012-13 spring data for each of the tests. Students in grades 3 through 8 take this test. **See Table B.2** for the means and standard deviations used to standardize these variables.
Core GPA	Core GPA is the combination of grades from English, math, science, and social studies classes in the elementary grades.
Survey Data	Rasch scale made from items collected through the *My Voice, My School* survey. The following measures were used in our analyses:
Student Measures	

Safety Measure: How safe do you feel:
- Outside around the school?
- Traveling between home and school?
- In the hallways of the school?
- In the bathrooms of the school?
- In your classes?

Student Classroom Behavior Measure: Most students in my school:
- Like to put others down
- Help each other learn
- Don't get along together very well
- Treat each other with respect

Student-Teacher Trust Measure: How much do you agree with:
- I feel safe and comfortable with my teachers at this school.
- My teachers always keep their promises
- My teachers will always listen to students' ideas?
- My teachers treat me with respect?

School Safety Measure: How much do you agree with the following statements about your school?
- I worry about crime and violence at this school
- Students at this school are often teased or picked on
- Students at this school are often threatened or bullied

Teacher Measures

Teachers Safety Measure:
To what extent is each of the following a problem at your school?
- Physical conflicts among students
- Robbery or theft
- Gang activity
- Disorder in classrooms
- Disorder in hallways
- Student disrespect of teachers
- Threats of violence toward teachers

Teacher-Teacher Trust Measure:
To what extent do you feel respected by other teachers at this school?
How much do you agree with the following statements about your school?
- Teachers in this school trust each other
- It's OK in this school to discuss feelings, worries, and frustrations with other teachers
- Teachers respect other teachers who take the lead in school improvement efforts
- Teachers at this school respect those colleagues who are experts at their craft

TABLE B.2
Test Score Means and Standard Deviations in 2012-13, by Grade

	ISAT		NWEA	
	Math	Reading	Math	Reading
Grade 3	209 (31.2)	200 (31.6)	200 (14.0)	193 (17.1)
Grade 4	225 (28.0)	212 (28.8)	210 (14.9)	202 (16.3)
Grade 5	235 (29.4)	224 (27.0)	217 (16.7)	207 (16.1)
Grade 6	250 (29.8)	236 (24.4)	221 (16.5)	212 (15.4)
Grade 7	260 (31.0)	239 (27.2)	226 (17.3)	216 (15.4)
Grade 8	271 (28.1)	247 (21.2)	230 (18.0)	219 (15.3)

TABLE B.3
List of Closed Schools and Welcoming Schools Affected by 2013 Closures

Closed School	Welcoming School(s)	Utilization Rate		2012-13 Performance Level	
		Closed	Welcoming	Closed	Welcoming
Altgeld	Wentworth	48%	41%	Level 3 (26%)	Level 3 (45%)
Armstrong	Leland	36%	81%	Level 2 (62%)	Level 1 (93%)
Banneker	Mays	49%	64%	Level 3 (43%)	Level 3 (45%)
Bethune	Gregory	48%	37%	Level 3 (36%)	Level 1 (81%)
Bontemps	Nicholson	46%	50%	Level 3 (17%)	Level 1 (81%)
Buckingham	Montefiore	54%	13%	Level 3 (31%)	Level 3 (39%)
Calhoun	Cather	46%	30%	Level 2 (69%)	Level 1 (76%)
Delano	Melody	37%	34%	Level 2 (55%)	Level 2 (62%)
Dumas	Wadsworth	36%	46%	Level 3 (26%)	Level 3 (45%)
Duprey	De Diego	28%	71%	Level 2 (50%)	Level 2 (57%)
Emmet	DePriest	66%	61%	Level 3 (48%)	Level 2 (57%)
	Ellington		43%		Level 1 (71%)
Fermi	South Shore	53%	79%	Level 3 (24%)	Level 3 (44%)
Garfield Park	Faraday	39%	47%	Level 3 (17%)	Level 1 (74%)
Goldblatt	Hefferan	30%	40%	Level 2 (69%)	Level 1 (74%)
Goodlow	Earle	60%	43%	Level 3 (31%)	Level 3 (36%)
Henson	C. Hughes	32%	56%	Level 3 (10%)	Level 2 (57%)
Herbert	Dett	44%	25%	Level 3 (38%)	Level 2 (52%)
Key	Ellington	57%	43%	Level 2 (50%)	Level 1 (71%)
King	Jensen	43%	45%	Level 3 (33%)	Level 1 (83%)
Kohn	Lavizzo	37%	61%	Level 3 (36%)	Level 1 (71%)
	L. Hughes		48%		Level 3 (48%)
	Cullen		68%		Level 2 (67%)
Lafayette	Chopin	36%	37%	Level 3 (26%)	Level 1 (76%)
Lawrence	Burnham	47%	89%	Level 3 (36%)	Level 2 (55%)
Marconi	Tilton	41%	39%	Level 3 (43%)	Level 2 (50%)
May	Leland	45%	81%	Level 3 (45%)	Level 1 (93%)
Mayo	Wells	59%	51%	Level 3 (26%)	Level 3 (26%)
Morgan	Ryder	31%	44%	Level 3 (33%)	Level 3 (36%)
Near North	Montefiore	53%	13%	Level 3 (17%)	Level 3 (39%)
Overton	Mollison	51%	44%	Level 3 (36%)	Level 3 (48%)
Owens	Gompers	68%	55%	Level 3 (27%)	Level 3 (43%)

Appendix B

TABLE B.3: *CONTINUED*
List of Closed Schools and Welcoming Schools Affected by 2013 Closures

Closed School	Welcoming School(s)	Utilization Rate		2012-13 Performance Level	
		Closed	Welcoming	Closed	Welcoming
Paderewski	Cardenas	30%	84%	Level 3 (45%)	Level 1 (77%)
	Castellanos		91%		Level 2 (52%)
Parkman	Sherwood	41%	55%	Level 3 (45%)	Level 2 (52%)
Peabody	Otis	47%	60%	Level 3 (48%)	Level 2 (69%)
Pershing West	Pershing East	27%	92%	Level 2 (52%)	Level 2 (60%)
Pope	Johnson	34%	58%	Level 3 (45%)	Level 2 (67%)
Ross	Dulles	37%	61%	Level 3 (31%)	Level 2 (64%)
Ryerson	Ward, L.	58%	55%	Level 2 (50%)	Level 2 (64%)
Sexton	Fiske	41%	41%	Level 2 (50%)	Level 2 (64%)
Songhai	Curtis	44%	53%	Level 3 (33%)	Level 2 (52%)
Stewart	Brennemann	41%	51%	Level 2 (64%)	Level 2 (67%)
Stockton	Courtenay	45%	85%	Level 3 (38%)	Level 2 (64%)
Trumbull	Chappell	54%	71%	Level 3 (43%)	Level 1 (88%)
	McPherson		63%		Level 2 (57%)
	McCutcheon		89%		Level 2 (67%)
Von Humboldt	De Diego	40%	71%	Level 2 (50%)	Level 2 (57%)
West Pullman	Haley	44%	61%	Level 3 (31%)	Level 2 (55%)
Williams ES	Drake	66%	35%	Level 3 (26%)	Level 3 (43%)
Williams MS	Drake	53%	35%	Level 3 (21%)	Level 3 (43%)
Woods	Bass	46%	41%	Level 3 (43%)	Level 2 (60%)
Yale	Harvard	27%	70%	Level 3 (29%)	Level 3 (43%)

Table B.4 displays the characteristics of students in grades K-7 who were enrolled in closed schools and designated welcoming schools as of May 2013.

TABLE B.4
Sample of Students

Students in Grades K-7 May 2013	Students in Closed Schools (10,708 Students)	Students in Designated Welcoming Schools (13,218 Students)
Black	88%	74%
Latino	10%	22%
Free/Reduced-Price Lunch	95%	92%
Students with Identified Disabilities	17%	15%
Old for Grade	16%	11%
ISAT Math Test Spring 2012 Meeting/Exceeding Standards	29%	41%

Methods

Our strategy to estimate the effects of school closures on different student outcomes is based on a difference-in-difference approach. This approach, detailed below, compares changes in student outcomes for students affected by closures relative to students in schools not affected by school closings in 2013. First, we describe how the comparison groups were selected, followed by the difference-in-difference approach.

Selecting a comparison group for students from closed schools. The comparison group was selected to be students from schools that were on the list of potential closures back in February 2013, but were not affected by any school action. At that time, the list was comprised of 129 elementary schools. After removing any school on that list affected by any school actions, the group was reduced to 49 schools. Of the 129 schools, obviously 47 closed at the end of the year and two phased out the following years. Four more schools were part of co-locations and five became turnaround schools at the end of that year. In addition, four schools were removed because they were still under consideration for closure until the Board voted in May 2013 and 18 of the 129 schools on the February list ended up being designated welcoming schools for some of the closed schools. **Table B.5** shows some of the school characteristics of these groups.

There were 14,734 students in grades K-7 enrolled in the 49 closed school comparison group elementary schools in May 2013. **Table B.6** shows the characteristics of these students and the students from closed schools. In terms of student characteristics, these two groups of students were very similar. These two groups of schools were serving mostly Black students, with similar percentages of students receiving free or reduced-price lunch, and receiving special education services. Their academic performance measured by test scores were similar, as well. And the neighborhoods where the students came from had, in both cases, high crime rates and high levels of unemployment.

Selecting a comparison group for students from designated welcoming schools. Designated welcoming schools were selected to be higher-rated schools based on the accountability rating given to schools in 2012-13 (the year of closing decisions), within a mile of closed schools, and enough seats to accommodate the students from closed schools. **Table B.7** shows that, on average, the 48 designated welcoming schools had a utilization rate of 54 percent, and 26 percent of the schools were rated Level 1 ("excellent standing"), 49 percent were rated Level 2 ("good standing"), and the rest were rated Level 3 ("on probation"). We selected the comparison group of schools to satisfy the same criteria as the designated welcoming schools: higher-rated than

TABLE B.5

Characteristics of the Schools Affected by Closings and the Comparison Group

	Number	Average Utilization Rate	Performance Level
			Level 1 – Level 2 – Level 3
Closed Schools	47	46%	0% — 24% — 76%
Comparison Schools	49	51%	0% — 27% — 73%

TABLE B.6

Characteristics of the Students Affected by Closings and the Comparison Group

	Students in Closed Schools (10,708 Students)	Students from Comparison Schools (14,734 Students)
Black	88%	84%
Latino	10%	13%
Free/Reduced-Price Lunch	95%	94%
Students with Identified Disabilities	17%	16%
Old for Grade	16%	15%
ISAT Math Test Spring 2012 Meeting/Exceeding Standards	29%	29%

TABLE B.7

Characteristics of the Schools Designated Welcoming Schools and the Comparison Group

	Number	Average Utilization Rate	Performance Level
			Level 1 – Level 2 – Level 3
Designated Welcoming Schools	48	54%	26% — 49% — 26%
Comparison Schools	73	65%	27% — 45% — 27%

TABLE B.8

Characteristics of the Students in the Designated Welcoming Schools and the Comparison Group

	Students in Designated Welcoming Schools (13,218 Students)	Students from Comparison Schools (25,947 Students)
Black	74%	66%
Latino	22%	26%
Free/Reduced-Price Lunch	92%	90%
Students with Identified Disabilities	15%	14%
Old for Grade	11%	11%
ISAT Math Test Spring 2012 Meeting/Exceeding Standards	41%	43%

closed ones and with enough capacity, but we selected those that were just beyond a mile (between 1 mile and 1.3 miles from closed schools). These schools were not selected to be designated welcoming schools because they were a bit farther from closed ones but they were similar to designated welcoming schools in the other characteristics.

We found 73 schools within the 1 to 1.3 mile distance, with an average utilization rate of 65 percent and similar distribution of performance levels as the designated welcoming schools. Characteristics of designated welcoming schools and the comparison schools are shown in **Table B.8**.

Figures B.1 through B.8 show the trends of the different student outcomes under study for students from closed schools and their comparison group (panel A) and students from designated welcoming schools and their comparison group (panel B). These graphs represent the unadjusted averages for students who were in the sample in a particular year.

FIGURE B.1

School Transfer Rates Over Time

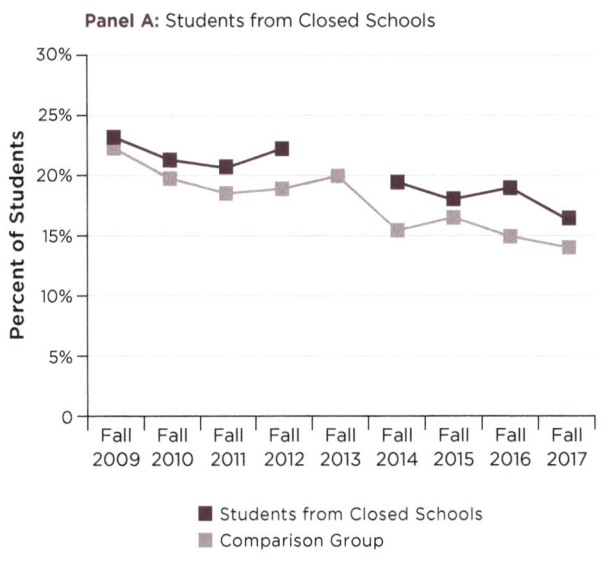
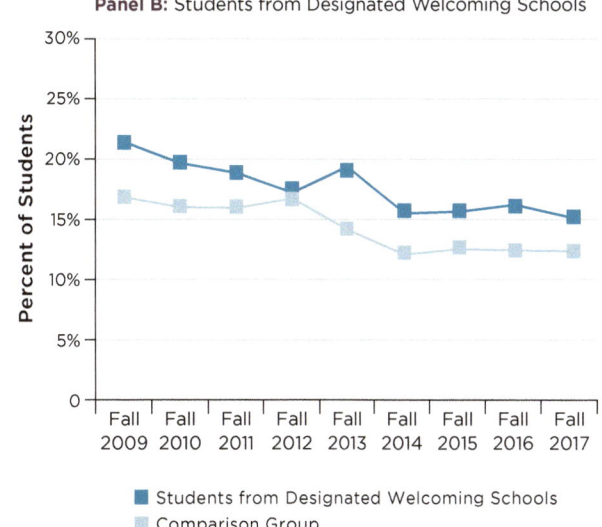

FIGURE B.2
Number of Days Absent Over Time

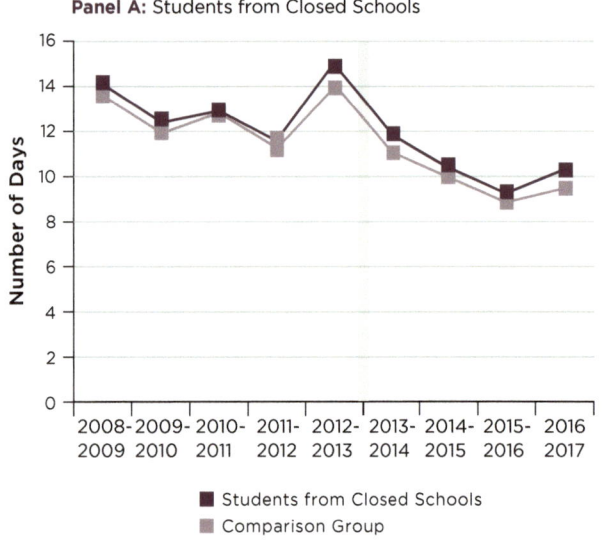
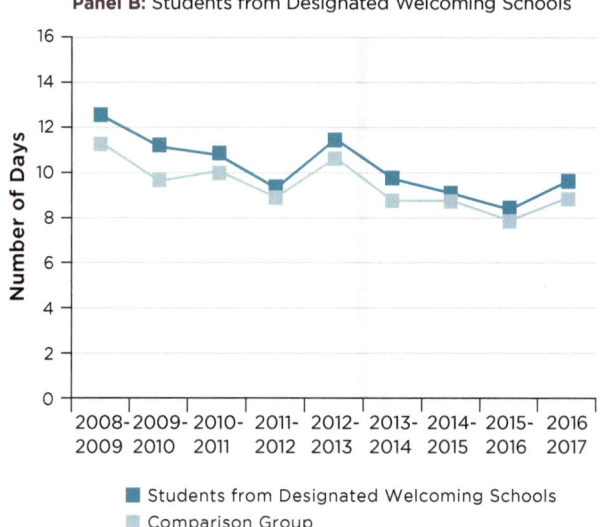

FIGURE B.3
Suspension Rates Over Time

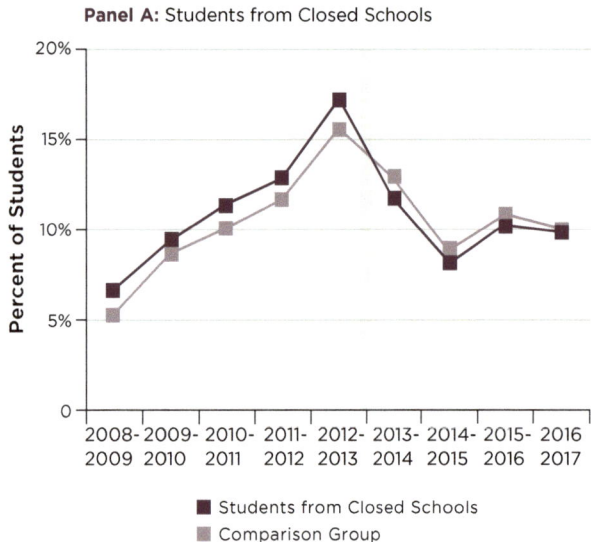
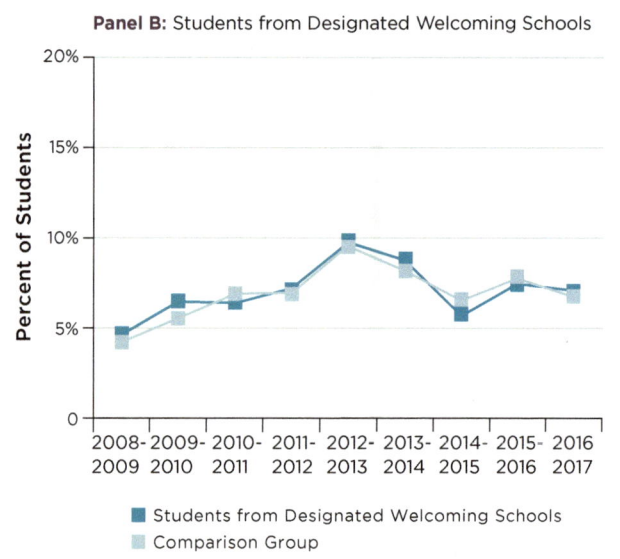

FIGURE B.4
Reading ISAT Test Scores Over Time

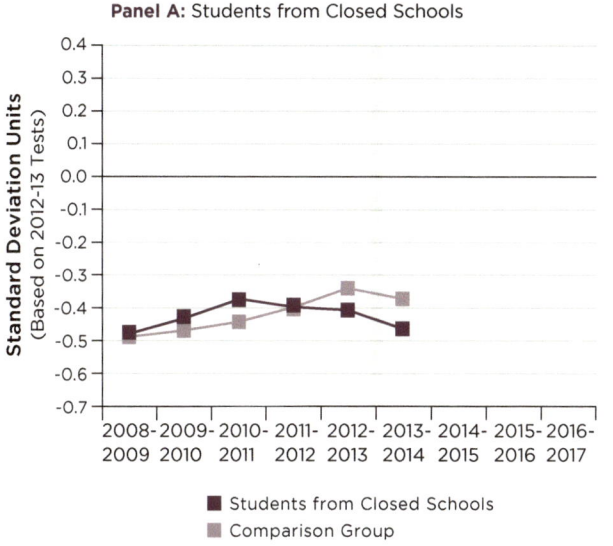
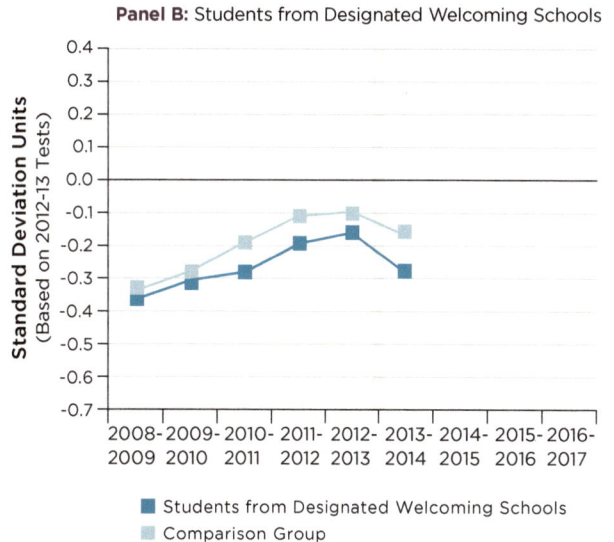

FIGURE B.5
Math ISAT Test Scores Over Time

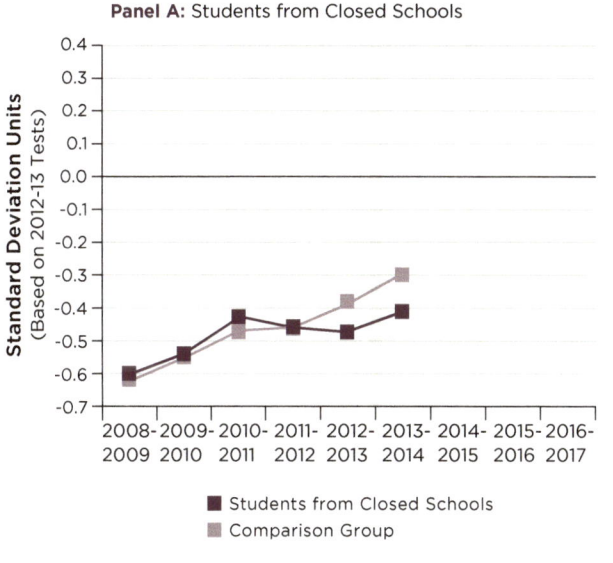
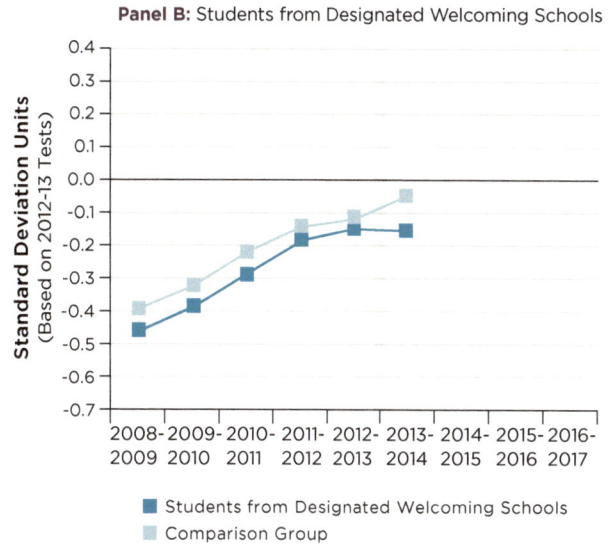

FIGURE B.6
Reading NWEA Test Scores Over Time

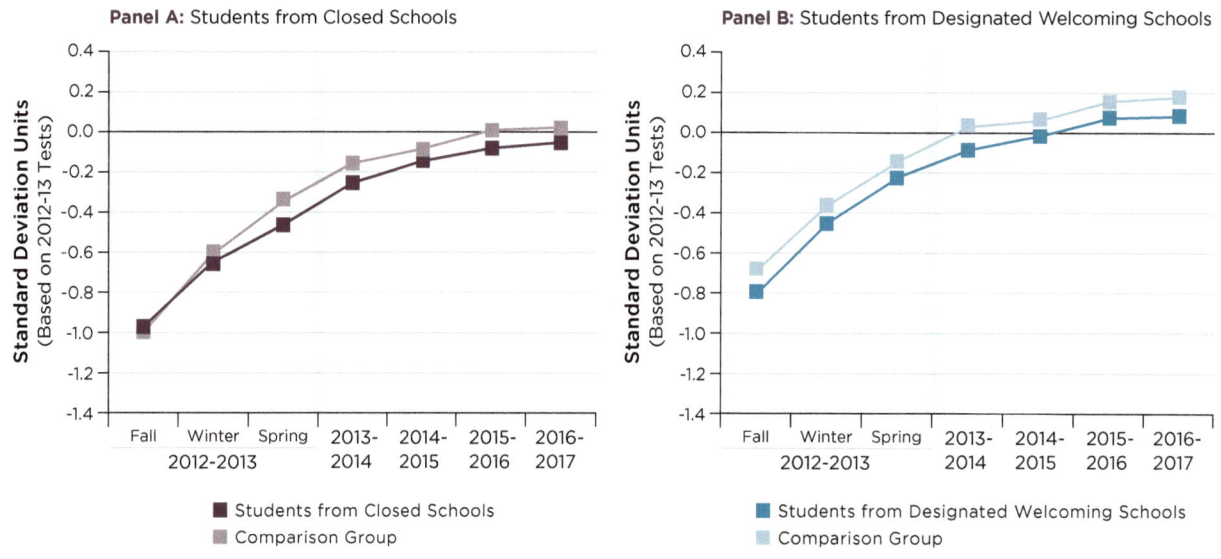

FIGURE B.7
Math NWEA Test Scores Over Time

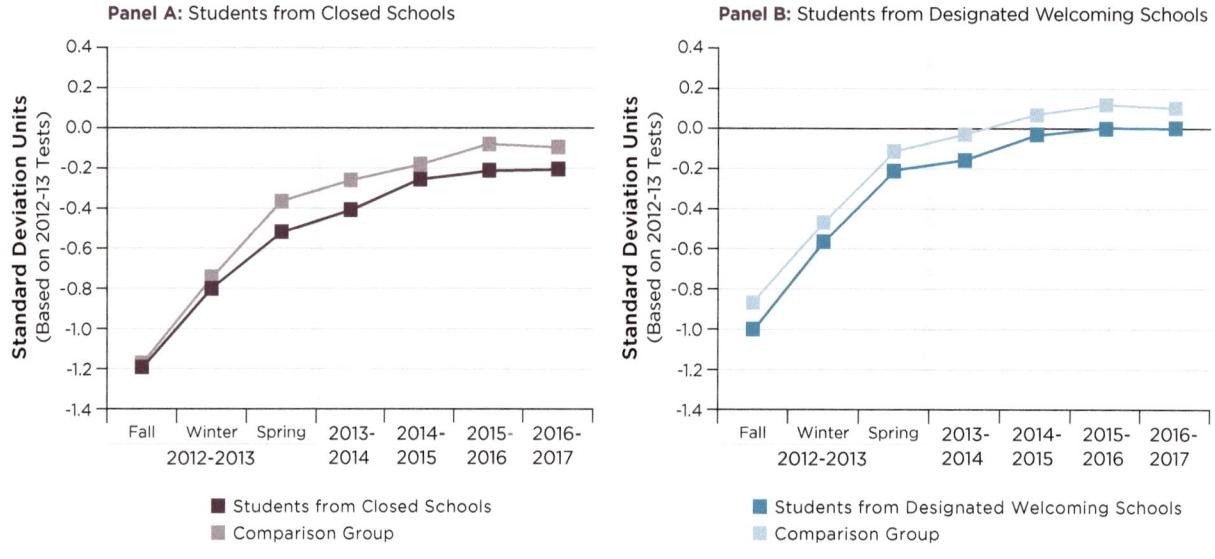

FIGURE B.8
Core GPA Over Time

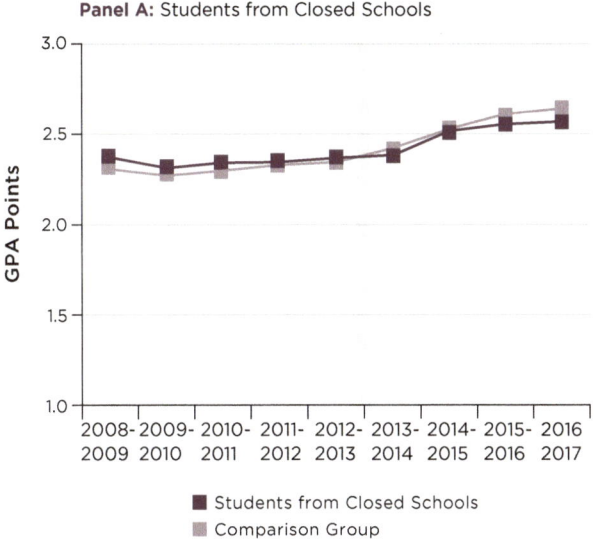

Model

The analyses of the impact on students from closed schools and designated welcoming schools was done separately but the model is the same. Equation 1 presents an estimation equation in which outcome Y for student *i* in time *t* is modeled as a function of indicators for time-varying student characteristics (X_{it}), year ($dYear_t$), an interaction of year with the affected group of students ($dYear_t \, dAffected_i$), and a series of dummy variables indicating the grade the student was at a particular year (ϕ_{it}), and an error term (ε_{it}).

$$Y_{it} = \alpha_i + \phi_{it} + \beta \, Y_{it} + \sum_{p=2009}^{2017} \rho_p \, dYear_t + \sum_{p=2009}^{2017} \delta_p \, dYear_t \, dAffected_i + \varepsilon_{it}$$

Instead of estimating a trend, we allow for a more flexible specification by including the set of yearly dummy variables. The interaction of the yearly dummy variables with the *dAffected* variable estimates the deviations in outcomes for the affected students with respect to the comparison group. We tested whether the set of interactions before the intervention (from 2009–12) were all equal to zero to ascertain whether the trends were similar in both groups pre-intervention.

The model also controls for an individual student-specific term (α_i), in effect measuring deviations in an outcome around the student's "average" performance level. In doing so, we can trace out whether student outcomes changed in the year or two prior to the announcement, and whether any differences after the announcement appeared immediately or gradually. This individual specific effect is fixed over time and takes account of any factors that are unchanging over time (such as an individual's level of scholastic ability, race, gender, or aspects of their home or neighborhood that are constant over time). Standard errors were clustered at the school year level.

By selecting schools for the control groups with the same criteria that CPS used to identify the treated schools, the schools in each control group should have had experiences similar to their respective treatment group school prior to the final closings announcement. The students and staff in the 49 schools in the closings control group should have experienced the same threat of closing as the 47 schools that actually did close, as both groups were on the same list up until the final announcement. Likewise, the students and staff in the 73 schools in the welcoming control group were in similar schools as the welcoming schools and they serve as a way of measuring how the students in welcoming schools should have fared in the absence of the merger of the student and teacher populations.

The validity of the estimates from our models to

represent the true effects of the schools closings announcement relies on the assumption that the outcomes for students in the treated and control schools followed a common trajectory through time and that the trajectory would have remained parallel in the absence of the policy to close schools. On the other hand, because the model is estimating the deviation from this common trend after the closings announcement, a causal interpretation does not rely on the assumption that the trend lines for each group are coincident—absolute differences between groups may exist. In other words, we are not estimating whether students in control schools have different outcomes than students in treated schools, but rather whether the difference in outcomes between the two groups increased or decreased after the closings announcement.

Tables B.9 and B.10 show the estimates for the models run for both groups of students.

TABLE B.9

Estimates for Students from Closed Schools

	Student Mobility	Absences	Suspensions	Core GPA	ISAT Reading	ISAT Math	NWEA Reading	NWEA Math
Pre-Intervention Years								
2008-09	-0.0210	0.0020	-0.0023	0.0289	0.0264	0.0138	—	—
2009-10	-0.0119	-0.0066	-0.0064	0.0248	0.0219	-0.0229	—	—
2010-11	-0.0059	-0.0173	0.0000	0.0133	0.0299	0.0167	—	—
2011-12	Reference							
Announcement Year								
2012-13	—	0.0499	0.0043	0.0098	-0.0670**	-0.1071***		
Fall							Reference	Reference
Winter							-0.0344	-0.0240
Spring							-0.1093**	-0.1227**
Post-Intervention Years								
2013-14	0.0166	0.0492	-0.0249	-0.0515	-0.0853**	-0.1054**	-0.0380	-0.0958*
2014-15	-0.0111	0.0081	-0.0165	-0.0256	—	—	-0.0228	-0.0535
2015-16	0.0161	0.0288	-0.0120	-0.0884*	—	—	-0.0441	-0.1185**
2016-17	-0.0016	0.0424	-0.0099	-0.1144**	—	—	-0.0449	-0.1081*
P-Value Test: Pre-Intervention Years Differences = 0								
	0.6727	0.9268	0.9575	0.8738	0.6393	0.6807	—	—
Number of Students								
	24,955	25,394	25,442	25,116	18,153	18,170	23,683	23,687
Number of Observations								
	132,474	158,039	158,803	138,163	61,219	61,179	102,814	102,945

Note: Significance levels: *** p<0.001; ** p<0.01; * p<0.05

TABLE B.10

Estimates for Students from Designated Welcoming Schools

	Student Mobility	Absences	Suspensions	Core GPA	ISAT Reading	ISAT Math	NWEA Reading	NWEA Math
Pre-Intervention Years								
2008-09	0.0514*	0.0721	-0.0002	-0.0496	0.0560	-0.0142	—	—
2009-10	0.0367	0.0814*	0.0066	-0.0064	0.0372	-0.0246	—	—
2010-11	0.0298	0.0233	-0.0035	0.0104	-0.0149	-0.0193	—	—
2011-12				Reference				
Announcement Year								
2012-13	0.0466*	-0.0142	0.0038	0.0091	-0.0129	0.0039		
Fall							Reference	Reference
Winter							0.0379	0.0432
Spring							0.0443	0.0388
Post-Intervention Years								
2013-14	0.0293	0.0400	0.0051	0.0074	-0.0846**	-0.0627	-0.0106	0.0055
2014-15	0.0245	-0.0257	-0.0082	0.0323	—	—	0.0164	0.0279
2015-16	0.0261	-0.0006	-0.0013	-0.0231	—	—	0.0086	-0.0036
2016-17	0.0114	0.0015	0.0037	-0.0049	—	—	-0.0167	-0.0088
P-Value Test: Pre-Intervention Years Differences = 0								
	0.1010	0.0486	0.6660	0.5593	0.1440	0.9166	—	—
Number of Students								
	38,739	39,081	39,165	37443	27955	27,965	36,759	36,767
Number of Observations								
	221,784	244,323	245,643	204,814	94,272	94,338	158,762	159,376

Note: Significance levels: *** $p<0.001$; ** $p<0.01$; * $p<0.05$

ABOUT THE AUTHORS

MOLLY F. GORDON is a Research Scientist at the University of Chicago Consortium on School Research. Her current research focuses on the impact of closing schools on families, students, and staff and examining preschool attendance improvement efforts. Previously, she was a Research Associate at the Center for Applied Research and Educational Improvement (CAREI) at the University of Minnesota. She earned a BA in philosophy and an MA in educational policy studies from the University of Wisconsin–Madison, and a PhD in educational policy and administration from the University of Minnesota–Twin Cities.

MARISA DE LA TORRE is a Senior Research Associate and Managing Director at the University of Chicago Consortium on School Research. Her research interests include urban school reform, school choice, and early indicators of school success. Before joining UChicago Consortium, de la Torre worked for the Chicago Public Schools in the Office of Research, Evaluation, and Accountability. She received a master's degree in economics from Northwestern University.

JENNIFER R. COWHY is a first-year PhD student in the School of Education and Social Policy at Northwestern University. Cowhy is interested in researching how schools can better serve students who have experienced adverse childhood experiences and students with IEPs. Cowhy worked at the Consortium for six years prior to beginning her studies at Northwestern and received her MPP and AM in social service administration from the University of Chicago and her AB in sociology from the University of Michigan.

PAUL T. MOORE was a Research Analyst at the University of Chicago Consortium on School Research at the time this research was conducted. He has substantial experience evaluating the impacts of education policies and is an expert in causal inference with quasi-experimental designs. His research interests include urban school reform, school choice policies and practices, and quasi-experimental design methodologies. Moore has studied historical trends in student performance and school quality in Chicago. He has co-authored a number of journal articles and reports.

LAUREN SARTAIN is a Senior Research Analyst at the University of Chicago Consortium on School Research. She has a BA from the University of Texas at Austin, as well as a master's degree in public policy and a PhD from the Harris School of Public Policy at the University of Chicago. She has worked at Chapin Hall and the Federal Reserve Bank of Chicago. Sartain's research interests include principal and teacher quality, school choice, and urban school reform.

DAVID J. KNIGHT is a PhD student in the Department of Political Science and a fellow in the Interdisciplinary Training Program in Education at the University of Chicago. His current research focuses on the political consequences of housing and education policy and the intersections of race, ethnicity, and place in the transition to adulthood in Chicago. Prior to coming to Chicago, Knight was a public school teacher in Boston. He earned an AB in history from Dartmouth College, trained as a teacher at Stanford University, and began his research career as a master's student at Harvard University.

This report reflects the interpretation of the authors. Although the UChicago Consortium's Steering Committee provided technical advice, no formal endorsement by these individuals, organizations, or the full UChicago Consortium should be assumed.

UCHICAGO Consortium on School Research

Directors

ELAINE M. ALLENSWORTH
Lewis-Sebring Director

CAMILLE A. FARRINGTON
Managing Director and Senior Research Associate

JULIA A. GWYNNE
Managing Director and Senior Research Scientist

HOLLY HART
Survey Director

KYLIE KLEIN
Director of Research Operations

BRONWYN MCDANIEL
Director of Outreach and Communication

JENNY NAGAOKA
Deputy Director

MELISSA RODERICK
Senior Director Hermon Dunlap Smith Professor School of Social Service Administration

PENNY BENDER SEBRING
Co-Founder

MARISA DE LA TORRE
Managing Director and Senior Research Associate

Steering Committee

RAQUEL FARMER-HINTON
Co-Chair
University of Wisconsin, Milwaukee

DENNIS LACEWELL
Co-Chair
Urban Prep Charter Academy for Young Men

Ex-Officio Members

SARA RAY STOELINGA
Urban Education Institute

Institutional Members

SARAH DICKSON
Chicago Public Schools

ELIZABETH KIRBY
Chicago Public Schools

TROY LARAVIERE
Chicago Principals and Administrators Association

KAREN G.J. LEWIS
Chicago Teachers Union

ALAN MATHER
Chicago Public Schools

TONY SMITH
Illinois State Board of Education

Individual Members

GINA CANEVA
Lindblom Math & Science

NANCY CHAVEZ
OneGoal

KATIE HILL
Office of the Cook County State's Attorney

MEGAN HOUGARD
Chicago Public Schools

GREG JONES
Kenwood Academy

PRANAV KOTHARI
Revolution Impact, LLC

LILA LEFF
Umoja Student Development Corporation & Emerson Collective

RITO MARTINEZ
Surge Institute

LUISIANA MELÉNDEZ
Erikson Institute

SHAZIA MILLER
NORC at the University of Chicago

CRISTINA PACIONE-ZAYAS
Erikson Institute

BEATRIZ PONCE DE LEÓN
Generation All

PAIGE PONDER
One Million Degrees

KATHLEEN CALIENTO
The Academy Group

AMY TREADWELL
Chicago New Teacher Center

REBECCA VONDERLACK-NAVARRO
Latino Policy Forum

PAM WITMER
Illinois Network of Charter Schools

JOHN ZEIGLER
DePaul University